A Flame
in the Shadows

Robert Reid, Bishop of Orkney
1541 – 1558

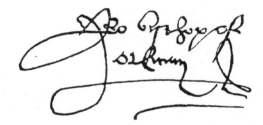

Olaf D. Cuthbert

First Published 1998
The Orkney Press Ltd
8 Broad Street
Kirkwall
Orkney KW15 1NX

ISBN No: 0 907618 48 0

Cover photograph by Tim Wright

This book was published with the assistance of a grant from the Orkney Islands Council

Printed by Chappell Gardener

01753 861848

To the memory of
Leon Nowosilkski
whose book this should have been
and of my parents
Margaret and Milroy
who brought me up a 'Catholic'
in a 'Protestant' church

Bishop Reid's Bookplate stamped on the covers of all his books
Photograph by courtesy of University of St. Andrews Library, Dept. of Manuscripts and Muniments

A colour reproduction of the above appears on page 100

Foreword

Robert Reid, Bishop of Orkney at the time of the Reformation, was, in the words of Professor Gordon Donaldson, "one of the outstanding churchmen of the century." Monk, priest, President of the Court of Justice, diplomat, builder of churches, Renaissance man of learning and piety, Bishop Reid was a man of his times, and also a man who transcended his times.

There has long been a need for a full study of this remarkable ecclesiastic, and Dr Olaf Cuthbert has more than met this need with this well-researched volume. Dr Cuthbert has followed up his perspicacious study of the Rev George Low, minister, naturalist and historian, with an impressive and learned account of the life and work of Robert Reid which will leave many people in his debt.

At a time when the leadership of the Catholic Church in Scotland largely failed to meet the turbulent challenges of the day, Robert Reid stands out as a Catholic Bishop who was true to his faith, both in doctrine and in life. From his seat at the Viking St. Magnus Cathedral, Reid was a doughty defender of the faith who impressed both his supporters and his enemies. If all of the bishops had been of Reid's calibre, the ecclesiastical history of Scotland might have been more than a little different.

Yet, as Olaf Cuthbert points out, many of Robert Reid's achievements were short lived. Within a year of his death, his successor as Bishop of Orkney had embraced the Reformed faith. The church of St. Olaf which he restored was abandoned. Had he lived longer, Robert Reid would have had much to weep about.

Dr Cuthbert's assessment is a balanced one: "Regardless of what develops in the future, the life of a man who keeps the faith, cares for others and seeks to leave the world in which he lived in a better state than he found it, has not lived in vain. Reid was loved and honoured by those who knew him and respected by those with whom he had official dealings, whether friend or enemy."

This is a fine book about a great, if flawed, figure who has left his mark on Orkney's - and Scotland's - history.

Rev. Ronald Ferguson, Minister, St. Magnus Cathedral,
St. Magnus Day, 1998.

Preface

Robert, bishop of Orkney, is a name that crops up throughout accounts of sixteenth century Scotland but I know of no published life of this remarkable cleric and statesman. Although I am neither a Scot nor an historian I hope that I will be forgiven for attempting to fill the gap. I have consulted a number of sources for information most of which are given in the bibliography at the end of the book. There is, however, one that requires special mention. On the advice of the historian, John Ballantyne, I consulted the thesis, written for a Ph.D. from the St. Thomas Aquinas University in Rome, by Father Leon Nowosilski, a member of the Polish Community of Marian Fathers. This thesis, now in the Department of Manuscripts of the National Library of Scotland, is entitled 'Robert Reid and His Times'. It is a detailed and extensively researched monograph on the man and the period, although only two of the seven chapters deals directly with Robert Reid. It is a scholarly work written for scholars. Fr. Nowosilski was meticulous in going, wherever possible, to contemporary sources which were often at odds with received wisdom. For the most part I have accepted his account in preference to other later works where the two differ. On only a few occasions have I felt it possible to disagree with his conclusions. I have made extensive use of his manuscript and the story he unfolds but have endeavoured to retell it in a way that may be more acceptable to the ordinary reader as opposed to the professional historian. As therefore this book is not intended as an historical thesis, I have kept notes to a minimum referring to direct quotations from works other than that of Fr. Nowosilski and in only a few instances making direct reference to Fr. Nowosilski's manuscript, although, on occasions I have used Fr. Nowosilksi's vivid descriptions, as for example at the marriage of Queen Mary, altering his words only to simplify the narrative. Anyone wishing to investigate his sources more fully would be advised to consult his manuscript in which he provides a great number of detailed references.

Sadly Fr. Nowosilski died twenty years ago and his monumental work has had little attention paid to it, although the late Gordon Donaldson, with whom he corresponded, regarded it as one of the finest pieces of historical research he had encountered.

It is for this reason that I have dedicated this book to his memory in the hope that he might achieve, posthumously, the recognition he deserves.

I am pleased to acknowledge a generous grant from the Scottish Arts Council toward the research and also a grant from the Orkney Heritage Society toward the translation of some medieval Latin manuscripts. This was meticulously carried out by Dr. Maxwell-Stuart of St. Andrews University, for which I am most grateful.

Dr. James Kirk of Glasgow University has been kind enough to allow me access to the archives of the History Department that deal with the Scots in Rome, derived from the Vatican archives. Dr. Kirk also advised me on the possible means of contacting the community of Marian Fathers in my quest for information regarding Fr. Nowosilski. I was able to benefit from the information to the extent of visiting the order of Marian Fathers at their house in Hereford where Father Nowosilski worked and pay my respects to his memory on a visit to Hereford Cemetery where he is interred. I was also in correspondence with Father Roman Przetak at the headquarters of the order, Fawley Court, Henley-on-Thames and received from him every courtesy and a supply of informative literature regarding the Marian Fathers.

As always I have received courteous assistance from the staff of the National Library of Scotland and from Dr. Norman Reid and his staff of the Manuscript Department of St. Andrews University. I have also received helpful advice and information from Dr. Peter Anderson, Deputy Keeper of Records, the National Registrar of Archives (Scotland).

I am also grateful to the staff of the Archives de France and those of the Archives Departmentales de la Seine-Maritime for their replies to my queries and to Miss Christina de Bellaigue in searching the records of the Archives de France on my behalf.

Monsieur Maurice Duteurtre, President des Amys du Vieux Dieppe, has been most helpful in replying to my request concerning the plaque to Robert Reid in the church of St. Jacques in Dieppe, the original of which is no longer in place. The Orkney Heritage Society with the co-operation of the Orkney Islands Council has since presented a facsimile of the original plaque and M. Duteutre and M. l'Abbe Vion kindly arranged for a ceremony to record its return to the chapel in the church of St. Jacques in Dieppe.

Apart from introducing me to Nowosilski's work, John Ballantyne has been kind enough to read the manuscript and I am indebted to him for his critical comments and advice.

I am particularly pleased that the Church of Scotland minister of St. Magnus Cathedral, the Reverend Ron Ferguson, agreed to write the

Foreword to this book. Whether or not he would endorse all that it contains, it is consistent with the ecumenical climate of our times that he is able to acknowledge the Christian witness of his distinguished predecessor despite any differing doctrinal values.

My publisher, Howie Firth, has given me much encouragement and advice.

Finally, as in all my endeavours, I am, as ever, in debt to my wife for her support and forbearance.

Contents

As a monk, Robert Reid would have regularly said or sung the daily offices of the church. Whilst the MASS was the central act of worship, the offices were adjuncts to it. They corresponded to the divisions of the day as computed by the Romans. Thus LAUDS was the first canonical hour of prayer said at daybreak; PRIME, the second, said at 6.00 a.m.; TERCE, the third, at 9.00 a.m.; SEXT, the fourth, at noon; NONE, the fifth, at 3.00 p.m.; VESPERS, the sixth, at 6.00 p.m. and COMPLINE, the seventh, said at the end of the day. MATINS, was originally a night office, said on the previous evening or with Lauds.

TENEBRAE was a combination of Matins and Lauds said or sung on the last three days of Lent, at which the candles were successively extinguished.

As these offices served to mark the divisions of Reid's day, they have been applied in this volume to mark the various periods of his life.

Illustrations

Introduction
Matins

Nisi Dominus aedificaverit domum, in vanum laboraverunt qui aedificant eam.
Nisi Dominus custodierit civitatem, frustra vigilat qui custodit eam.

In the autumn of 1558 in a humble lodging house in the French port of Dieppe, there was acted out a parable of the Scottish Reformation. Two men, old friends and colleagues, who had long debated their differing religious convictions held their last conversation. Both had been unwell. One was recovered, the other dying. In a last attempt to prevail on his friend to accept the inevitable triumph of his doctrine, the younger, fitter man begged his colleague to consider his immortal soul, so soon to face its maker. The dying man protested that it was too late to for him to discard all he had given his life to uphold and that he would await his end to see whether or no his faith had been justified. Nor would he be persuaded to move to more luxurious quarters. Too many of his church's leaders had put material considerations before spiritual ones, he would die where he was among his humbler friends. And so Robert Reid, bishop of Orkney, defender of the catholic faith, passed away and Lord James Stewart, prior of St. Andrew's, "Il Bastardo Scozia', King James V illegitimate son, returned to Scotland and took his place as one of the Lords of the Congregation.

This episode illustrates how the century in which they lived was both an end and a beginning.

It was a time when dark clouds hung over the medieval church. Yet, whilst Robert, bishop of Orkney, lived, one candle flame, at least, had kept at bay the encroaching shadows. It was perhaps fortunate for him that this light was extinguished before the darkness of that age finally closed in and a new age began.

Historians have written at length on the causes of the Reformation. There was however one over-riding cause and that was the very nature of the medieval church itself. From the earliest days of Christianity men had held that all men, and women, were equal in the sight of God. What they soon came to realise was that they are not equal in the sight of man.

Inevitably the infant church had to organise itself to take account of this. A hierarchy had to be established. A hierarchy, or its head, has to lay down rules of conduct and sooner or later it has to ensure that those rules are kept. The very name of the Roman Catholic church defined its status. 'Roman' since it founded its structure on the debris of the fallen Roman empire (even its early places of worship were the Roman basilicas) and 'catholic', that is 'universal', in that it embraced the whole of western 'Christendom'. To maintain its universality it needed to build a wall around itself and to allow of no dissent within. Schools arose in the medieval world in which men of learning disputed, often vehemently, but about the interpretation of dogma and the minutiae of theological meanings. They were not fools but they were bound by the church's teaching without either the freedom or wherewithal to question the basis of that teaching or to venture beyond it. When any such questioning did occur it was stamped upon by the burning of heretics or by waging war, as on the Albigensians in Provence.

It was as if a dyke had been built to keep out the sea of paganism and heresy. Occasionally a small breach would occur only to be hurriedly repaired. But such breaches weaken the structure and eventually as the seas get stronger and pressures well up from within, the weakened dyke gives way and, before it can be repaired or a new wall built, the whole countryside is flooded.

One of the waves that effected a breech in the wall was the advance of Islam. Whereas the crusades had resulted in the banding together of the Christian nations against the 'infidel' now the success of Islam in accomplishing the fall of Constantinople in 1453 had resulted in a flood of scholars seeking refuge in the west and bringing with them the inheritance of ancient Greece. This did not turn men into pagans but it did promote a release from the accretions of dogma that had restricted their thoughts. It revealed the existence of a philosophy unbound by those dogmas and it incited thinkers to look back, not just to the ancient writings of their Greek and Roman ancestors but to the very scriptures themselves and to view them anew, stripped of the rigid interpretations accorded them by centuries of ecclesiastical imprimatur. It has been suggested that an even earlier event started the rot. The Black Death that swept Europe in the mid fourteenth century was believed by many to be a punishment from God for their transgressions. Churchmen preached to that effect but churchmen were among the most affected which set men to question the basis of their authority.

At he same time petty kingdoms and loose confederations were developing into nation states demanding greater autonomy from the 'universal church' and the schools of the medieval world were coalescing into universities promoting greater exchanges of opinion.

As if that were not enough the invention, in the mid fifteenth century, of movable type for the printing of books, resulted in the a much wider dissemination of these opinions and, crucially, of Holy Scripture.

If the new learning engendered in men a new attitude to the faith it did not necessarily require them to abandon their centuries old allegiance to the church. It did however cause many to cry out for its reform. It was the church's tragedy that too many ignored the call, even when it came from some of its most devoted adherents.

Meanwhile there was a rising revulsion at the corruption of many of the church's institutions and at the cynical exploitation of the superstitions of simple men in order to finance the profligacy of the Holy See.

The Middle Ages reached their zenith with the High Renaissance under the patronage of popes who cared more for enriching their churches with works of art, their city with great architecture and themselves with palaces and possessions than for the spiritual needs of the masses whose father they professed to be. It took an obscure Augustinian friar in a small German town to put into words the feelings of the many who had become disillusioned with the path down which Christendom was being led.

Between these two forces, the new freedom of thought from without and the corruption within, the dyke finally gave way. Islands of Catholicism remained, some of the land was even reclaimed, but the damage was done, the 'catholic' church was no longer universal.

Too late the hierarchy of that church became conscious of the peril to which its conduct had been leading it. To counter the tide of Reformation a more austere papacy promoted the Counter Reformation. It was something long overdue and, although obtaining a partial success, it came too late to stem the tide of Protestant reform. European Christendom would never be the same again.

Such monolithic institutions are inherently unstable because in the end, whether after decades or centuries the mind of man, however fallible, needs to work out its own destiny. (We have witnessed a very similar occurrence in our own day. Communism too believed in the equality of man, it too needed a hierarchy to bring order into potential chaos. It too put up its dykes to keep the rest of the world from contaminating the teachings of the faithful and allowed no dissent. It too, when *perestroika* and *glasnost* finally breached its dyke and let the rest of the world flood in, collapsed beneath the tidal wave of western capitalism.)

If its hegemony had been shattered in Europe the Roman church nevertheless found new worlds to conquer as the adventurous spirit of man set out to discover new continents. Despite its initial defeat in many parts of Europe it is today still the most populous church in Christendom. There are signs, however, that the seas are getting rougher once more and that the waves of 'liberation theology' are threatening anew its outlying defences.

Scotland, on the northern edge of the continent, was to be affected by the tide later than most of the other countries of Europe. By the time the new movement reached it the country was ripe for reform. Its own archbishops, bishops and senior clergy were showing signs of the same degeneracy that had affected the papacy. Moreover it was not just religion that was demanding to be reformed but the political structure with which religion was so closely bound up. For the past hundred years or more an increasingly educated laity had begun to take over from the clergy many aspects of education and government, that had previously been the prerogative of churchmen. The church's unwillingness to surrender its hold over affairs of state added to the growing demand for reform in both church and state.

There remained some among the clergy however who, sympathetic to much of the teaching of the reformers, still struggled to maintain the dignity and purpose of their calling and to uphold the teachings of the catholic faith without hypocrisy and to work both for the good of mankind and the well-being of the state. Just such a man was Robert Reid. Though successful in his lifetime he, and those like him, had been born too late to present their church in a manner acceptable to the reforming spirit of the age.

Nevertheless it has been men of intellect and faith such as these, of many different creeds and cultures, who, through the ages, have kept, or attempted to keep, mankind from falling beneath the weight of its inherent selfishness. Robert Reid became one of the outstanding personalities of his time not because he made history, he did not, but because he went with history adding to it the flavour of his personality, which he was able to bring to bear on those who did indeed make history and to lighten the lives of those for whom that history, for good or ill, was being made.

It is important to be clear about one thing. The medieval church, despite the apparent materialism and venality of so many of its members was, at the same time, an intensely spiritual church. Men who might behave with cruelty toward their neighbours, spawn a dozen illegitimate children and amass fortunes at the expense of their weaker brethren nevertheless believed unquestionably in the virgin birth, the resurrection and the ascension, not as allegories but as facts. At the mass they partook of the flesh and blood of the Christ; the liturgy was as much an essential part of their lives as any other daily function and far more important. To enter into the house of the Lord was to be uplifted and to add meaning to an otherwise often very humdrum existence. If many were ignorant of the scriptures and aware only of what the priest chose to tell them, they took comfort in the ritual and sonorous Latin of the service. The clergy who intoned that Latin and the choirs that filled church, abbey and cathedral with heavenly sound were all taking part in the giving of solace and spiritual refreshment to a people whose lives would have been drab and meaningless otherwise. The clergy themselves, in spite of all their shortcomings, served their congregations in the sincere belief and knowledge that they were offering them the comfort of the Holy Spirit.

Not that there were not intellectuals among them but theirs was largely an intellect in thrall to dogma. Nor were there lacking men of great spirituality among the reformers but they, in turn, were too often limited by the austerity of their convictions. Those reformers who adopted a more spiritualistic approach to reform often found themselves persecuted by their more orthodox Protestant brethren.

Robert Reid was a servant of the medieval church and was, as such, a man of profound spirituality. He was also a man of intellect. He made use of the former to enhance the prestige of a faltering Catholicism and of the latter to forward the interests of the state. How far he succeeded and how far he failed in his endeavours may perhaps become apparent in this account of his life.

1 Lauds

Deus, Deus, ad te de luce vigilo
Sitivit in te anima mea, quam multipliciter tibi caro mea

i. Early years

When, in the autumn of 1513, Thomas Howard, succeeded in turning the flank of the Scots, and the English halberds proved more lethal than the clumsy Scottish spears, much of the flower of Scotland lay slain on the field of Flodden. Many children became fatherless that day; two of them, distant in rank and birth, were to become greatly dependent upon one another in later years. The younger, not yet two years of age, assumed the crown of Scotland as James the fifth; the elder would have to wait for his preferment but, in time, was to become a scholar, abbot, bishop, judge, ambassador and diplomat and even marriage-broker to two monarchs.

Exactly when Robert Reid was born is not known. He is recorded as having entered the university of St. Andrews in 1511. Students in the sixteenth century would normally begin their university career at any age between twelve and fifteen years, thirteen being quite normal. It must be assumed then that Robert was born sometime near the end of the last decade of the previous century, the year 1498 being as likely as any. His father, John Reid, lived at Aikenhead in Clackmannanshire on the north bank of the Black Devon, 2 miles north-east of Clackmannan. Little is known of John Reid except that he was charged with the murder of one Robert of Methven in Tillycultrie but was acquitted on the plea of self-defence. He was probably a fairly substantial laird since he was able to acquire a wife from a family of well-to-do landholders. It is to his mother and his mother's family that Robert probably owed most and from whom he acquired his religion, his learning and, above all, his character. Elizabeth Schanwell, more often known as Besseta, was the daughter of Duncan and Margaret Schanwell who owned the lands of Schanwell in the barony of Burn. They are known to have had at least four children, three sons and a daughter. John, the eldest son, became Abbot of Coupar-Angus in Fife in 1480; William, the second, a secular clerk, had a half lease in the church of Fossoway for five years from 1485; finally there was Robert who had a distinguished academic career. He matriculated at St. Andrew's in 1488 and graduated in 1492; was Chaplain of Corso in 1496 and Vicar of Kirkcaldy in 1501; Dean of the faculty of Arts in 1512 and 1517; Rector of St. Andrew's University in 1517-18 and Deputy Rector in 1518-19 and also Visitor of St. Salvator's College in 1518 and commissary of St. Andrew's in 1517-1520 and, in all, spent 35 years at St. Andrew's. In 1532 he was chosen to be a Justice of the Supreme Court, although he never took up the post, and in 1524 was Notary of Kirkcaldy.

Besseta Schanwell bore her husband six children of whom Robert was the third. After Flodden the eldest son, David, inherited his father's estate, later to be succeeded by his son John after David's death at the Battle of Pinkie in 1547. John married Katherine Dumbrek, one of two sisters the daughters of Thomas Dumbrek of that ilk (Dumbrek was in the parish of Udny). Thomas was the last of his line and died in 1550. The other daughter, Margaret, married George Halyburton.

The second son, James, married Euphemia Dundas, a staunch Catholic who once described John Knox as 'ane common harlot all his dayis'. Euphemia's son, Walter, was a favourite nephew of his uncle, Robert, who was to do much for the boy and fortunately, perhaps, did not live to see his expectations of him disappointed. James and Euphemia also had a daughter, Catherine, who married Alexander Dunbar, later dean of Moray. After Robert, Besseta bore three daughters, Christian who married Sir Edward Bruce and whose son became Lord Kinloss after the Reformation; Helen who married William Blackwood and Margaret.

It is not known when Besseta died but it is to be hoped that she lived to be proud of her son, who took full advantage of what she and his uncles were able to teach him.

How much influence his uncle John, the Abbot of Coupar-Angus, had on his nephew is uncertain, as he died in 1506 when Robert was only about eight years old. Uncle Robert, however, for whom, no doubt, he had been named, must have had great influence on the boy, supervising, as he would have done, his education at the University. All the young Robert's upbringing and education was directed toward inculcating in him the immutable truths of the catholic faith. These were to be his guiding light throughout his life and at the hour of his death.

In 1511, possibly at the age of 13 years, the young Robert Reid began his studies at St. Salvator's College in the University of St. Andrew's. Within two years, encouraged no doubt by his Uncle Robert and through his own application and intellect, he had progressed sufficiently to take his batchelor's degree in Arts. 1513 was the year in which he lost his father in battle with the English. This was a battle that the Scots had, regrettably, brought upon themselves by an ill-considered incursion over the border. It had been a half-hearted attempt to divert the English in support of their French allies with whom the English king, Henry VIII, was at the time in conflict.

Two years later studying under a famous theologian, Master Hugh Spens of St. Salvator's College, Reid took his masters degree being placed fifth. He was then elected an examiner of freshmen in the Faculty of Arts. There can never have been any doubt as to the career the young Robert Reid would follow. Younger sons, who had no property to inherit, had a limited choice. For a young man of intelligence and learning the church offered the prospect of advancement in a number of fields directly or indirectly connected with their vocation.

The year 1517, when Martin Luther nailed his thesis, deploring the sale of indulgences, to the door of his church, is often regarded as the start of the Reformation but the seeds of reform had been sown many years earlier.

It was during Reid's most impressionable years as a student and young cleric that the printed word began to flood into Scotland from Germany and the Low Countries with whom Scotland had close commercial ties. Many of these books carried the teachings of Martin Luther and the other reformers and, from south of the border, came copies of Tyndale's translation of the New Testament. Later the Acts of 1525 and of 1535 and their extension in 1541 forbade the dissemination of Bibles in the vernacular. The 1535 Act required any such books to be handed in to the bishops within forty days and, no doubt, many later passed through the hands of Reid both as abbot and bishop and were maybe added to his personal library. That they failed to change his beliefs is obvious but they may well have encouraged him to work toward an internal reformation of his church that would render the threatened Protestant reformation superfluous. Nor was he the only one to reach such a conclusion, Archbishop Hamilton who succeeded Cardinal Beaton at St. Andrew's and Robert Wauchope, who was prominent at the Council of Trent and brought its decrees to the Scotland, were two of the most prominent churchmen seeking to bring a measure of reform to the Scottish church. Their efforts were to prove to be too little and too late.

There had, of course, been earlier attempts at reform such as those of the Lollards in England and the Hussites in Bohemia but both these movements had greater influence in the lands of their birth and did not export well. Nevertheless they sowed seeds which the later reformers were able to harvest.

Apart from the abuses that men saw in the conduct of the clergy, which alone might not have been sufficient to bring about revolution in the church for, after all, such abuses were nothing new, there were theological questions being asked which were new. The whole purpose of life on earth was to prepare for eternal bliss in the life to come. Both the church of Rome and the reformers laid emphasis on the Passion as the means of salvation which would lead to that bliss. Where they differed was not in God's part but man's. God had sent His son to die on the cross and open the gates of heaven to the sinner; man questioned the way in which he should respond to that act. While Rome placed the Mass, as a re-enactment of the Passion, as the essential path to man's redemption, a passport to heaven for both the living and the dead (and more especially for the latter since the living can still redeem themselves by their deeds on earth); the reformers saw salvation not in a man's deeds but in his faith.

'A man is justified by faith without the deeds of the law' wrote St. Paul (Rom. ii. 28) and 'being justified by the faith, we have peace with God' (Rom. v.1). Doing good without faith, they believed, was no longer a possible path to salvation and any number of masses for the souls of the dead would avail nothing for the faithless. According to the later reformers even faith might be insufficient, only the Elect, those predestined by God, would achieve salvation. The Mass was to become a blasphemy.

None of this was acceptable to Robert Reid. Reform of the church and its ministers was one thing but a revolution in faith and practice as preached by the reformers was no better than conversion to Islam. Fifteen hundred years of tradition and revelation had built an edifice that was not to be destroyed by vandals just because a few essential repairs were required in an ageing building, however long overdue those repairs might be. His church's essential architecture was as beautiful as that of the real buildings, the cathedrals and abbeys, in which its ceremonies took place. Though both were in need of constant care and attention, which was often neglected, it was surely not too late to set about the repairs. Alas, it was, and, before his untimely death, he may have come to realise it.

ii. Clerk in Holy Orders

Although nepotism was an acceptable means of advancement, Reid's progress from now on no doubt owed every bit as much to his own abilities as to his family connections. A year after taking his masters degree he was appointed public notary to the diocese of Moray. From 1519 to 1521 he was back in Fife, acting in court as procurator for parties there and was also public notary by sacred Apostolic authority and styled a 'cleric of St. Andrew's'.

It is reported by many authorities that following his time at St. Andrew's Reid completed his education studying law at the University of Paris. It would have been a perfectly natural thing for him to have done and later commentators no doubt believed that a man who reached such eminence in the legal profession must naturally have taken this course. However there is no record of Reid's name among the register of students in the university archives and although there are some gaps in the records for the years 1492 to 1521, Nowosilski believes that the absence of Reid's name from the procurator's book for 1521-1525 and the receptor's book for 1515-1529 together with the fact he was fully occupied at home following his graduation from St. Andrew's in 1515, indicates that he could not have been in Paris at this time. It has been suggested that it was as a student in Paris that he met Giovanni Ferrerio but this too is unlikely since the Italian only arrived there in 1525 at which time Reid was busy in Moray. In favour of the belief that he studied law in Paris must be put the fact that Reid became a highly efficient lawyer well versed in both civil and canon law eventually achieving the highest legal position in the land (he was later to insist that all young students should study law at a "flourishing university"). It is difficult to understand how he reached such eminence as a lawyer without any formal training, although, as an exceptionally talented young man, it may be that he acquired his knowledge of the law from books, of which he was known to be a collector and an avid reader. He would also have gained experience by attendance at the many judicial hearings that came his way as a notary in Moray, procurator in Fife and later as official of Moray.

On 31st January 1523, as cleric of St. Andrew's and an M.A., he requested and was given by the then Pope, Adrian VI, the dispensation to hold two benefices and to demit them for two others when it should please him. Pope Adrian died in 1523 having been pontiff for barely one year and the confirmation of the dispensation was made by his successor Clement VII in November 1523. (Appendix 1)

It was in 1523 that Patrick Hamilton returned to Scotland and settled in St. Andrew's where he openly discussed Lutheran views with the young canons and students. Reid who still had close association with the university could scarcely have avoided becoming acquainted with Hamilton's teaching and may well have entered into discussion with him. Hamilton seems to have impressed all those with whom he came in contact. Gavin Logie, the principal of St. Leonard's College and John Winram, the sub-prior, were both receptive to his arguments and even John Major who had just arrived from Glasgow did not prevent his students from hearing his views and making up their own minds. Nevertheless his favourable reception did not prevent him being summoned by Archbishop James Beaton, possibly at the instigation of his nephew, David, to face a charge of heresy which forced his return to the continent. After publishing a thesis at Marburg that came to be known as 'Patrick's Places' he returned once more to Scotland to continue his teaching but in 1528 he was arrested, tried and burnt for heresy. Reid may have listened to Hamilton's views but clearly he was not prepared to abandon the tradition in which he had been brought up, even though he may have been prepared to take account of some of the new ideas emanating from the continent.

In 1524 or 1525 Robert Schanwell resigned the vicarage of Kirkcaldy and on the 22nd August 1525 the Pope, Clement VII, wrote to Robert Reid addressing him as 'perpetual vicar of the parish of Kirkcaldy' granting the vacancy to Reid provided any impediment to the provision could be overcome (there may have been some objection made). At the same time the pope informed him that he might also hold the subdeanery of Moray, in which office he succeeded William Winchester, and the 'vicarial duties in perpetuity of the vicarages of Grandtully and Drumdelgy' (Appendix 1). As subdean he was styled prebendary of Auldearn and in 1527 he is also referred to as official of Moray. The mandate was conveyed to Reid by the bishops of Casserta and Moray and Gilbert Strachan, canon of Aberdeen on 15th May 1526.

Bishop Robert Schaw of Moray, it is believed, had been thinking of choosing Reid as his successor but died before he could make the recommendation. It was a sad day for the diocese of Moray for, instead of Reid who would have filled the post with distinction, Schaw was succeeded first by Alexander Stewart who, in turn, was followed by Patrick Hepburn, uncle to the Earl of Bothwell the future husband of Queen Mary, and a man notorious for his loose living. Moray's loss was eventually to be Orkney's gain. In 1526 the possibility of a different preferment arose which was to present Reid with an appointment in which he would be able to exercise all his considerable talents.

iii. Preferment

What of the younger of the two children left fatherless by Flodden? Scotland after the battle once more inherited a monarch too young to govern. It seems to have been the fate of that unhappy country to have to suffer recurrent chaos resulting from the minority of its rulers. This occasion was no exception. The country required a governor and powerful lords flexed heir muscles for the coming contest for power. The first and most obvious choice for governor was John, Duke of Albany, grandson of James II. He was recalled from France and, despite being able to speak only French, proved successful for a time with the support of the next in line for the throne, James Hamilton, Earl of Arran. Most of the trouble for the governor arose, during the following years, from the Douglas family, one of whose members, the earl of Angus, had married the widowed queen, Margaret. However Queen Margaret was soon to discard Angus and become an enemy of the Douglases. Trouble arose from the rival claims of those who supported the French alliance and those, like the Douglases, who favoured an association with the English. The result of all this rivalry was to place the young king in the position of a pawn to be seized by one party or the other in order to obtain a temporary advantage. When Albany withdrew to France in 1524, the Earl of Arran, in agreement with the queen mother, invested the thirteen year old king with the symbols of sovereignty. From then on the king was theoretically in a position to make his own recommendations to the Pope in respect of ecclesiastical appointments. However it was not until 1528 that, freed from the domination of the Douglases, he was able to assume that responsibility. Yet it may be that in 1527, he did have some say in advancing the career of that other child who had been made fatherless at Flodden.

Monasteries had been established throughout Scotland in increasing numbers since the days of St. Margaret and her son David. Founded by royal piety, they had become centres of prayer and contemplation, the bedrock of the catholic faith in Scotland. In recent centuries however expediency had overtaken piety and many appointments of abbots and priors had become gifts of the king to his favoured courtiers or his inconvenient illegitimate offspring. Age or learning or indeed any inclination to the religious life often became, in these circumstances, largely irrelevant. Although many such appointments proved harmless, as the incumbents exercised their talents elsewhere and left the running of their monasteries to subordinates, some were disastrous and yet others surprisingly successful. Where monastic appointments were made from among the monks themselves or from men with a real vocation for the religious life then many monasteries continued to perform the services for which they were originally founded, with diligence and propriety.

St. Benedict established his rule in Italy in the sixth century bringing monks into communities where they could share a life of regular prayer and work. The Benedictine rule spread throughout the catholic world and by the eleventh century its rule was being adapted by individual monks to found their own communities on specific lines suited to varying requirements. One such monk named Robert left his community to found a new one at Citeaux near Dijon in France. The Cistercians, as the new community came to be called, followed the Benedictine rule strictly and laid stress on the virtue of manual work. In 1136 the Cistercians arrived in Scotland and founded a community at Melrose. Four years later other communities were founded from Melrose, among them that at Kinloss.

In 1526 the twenty-second abbot of Kinloss, Thomas Crystal, realising that he was dying, determined to find a successor who would continue the work he had started. Since his appointment as abbot in 1500 Crystal had done much for the monastery of Kinloss. He had improved the buildings, supplying annexes, kitchens and other buildings, repairing the roof of the church, restoring the chapel of St. James and adding three altars and two horologues. He also built houses at Ellon and Seyton and recovered property which had been appropriated by outsiders. He increased the income of the monastery, and was thereby enabled to increase the number of monks to twenty. He reformed the monastic observances and supported the intellectual life of the community by adding to the monastic library, for which he also required his named successor to bring books from France. He had supplied the king with apples and plums from the monastery garden and in return the king had renounced the salmon and other fishing on the river Findhorn. He was anxious therefore that all the hard work he had undertaken to advance the status of Kinloss as a place of religious devotion and learning should be maintained after he had departed. He was suffering from dropsy which forced his retirement (he was also said to have tumours of the legs and feet but this was probably just the swelling of the dropsy). He died at

Strathisla on 20th December 1535, almost a decade after his retirement, and was buried in the tomb he had constructed at Kinloss.

After considering a good number of possible candidates to fill the post he was about to vacate, Abbot Crystal finally came to accept that, in the young sub-dean of Moray, he had found the man he wanted.

As sub-dean of the Moray Diocese, Robert Reid would have been expected to be involved in settling disputes between members of the church. One such dispute arose in 1526, between the monastery of Cambuskenneth and the Vicar of Stirling, over the teind-salmon fished out of the Forth. The sub-dean, the official of St. Andrew's and the provost of St. Salvator's were commissioned by the pope to settle the matter after the abbot had appealed to the Holy See. In the event Reid and the official were able to leave the matter in the hands of the provost who acted for all three in this case. That Reid was able to get the provost to act in his name indicates something of the influence he was able to exert. It also shows that his name was already known to the papal authorities as a young man of learning and administrative ability.

In medieval times it had been the custom for the election of a new abbot to be undertaken by the monks. The methods used are as described by Mark Dilworth, in 'Scottish Monasteries in the late Middle Ages'[1] were:

1. Via Spiritus Sancti (way of the Holy Spirit) a name was said aloud and there was either acclamation or consenting silence.

2. Via compromisi (way of compromise): a person or persons were chosen, usually an odd number to avoid a split decision, and it was agreed that their choice would be accepted.

3. Via scrutini (way of scrutiny): a few monks were chosen and went aside; each declared his choice, then each of the other monks came singly and told them his choice. A notary recorded each vote.

By the sixteenth century, however, bishops and abbots of the major foundations were being nominated by the crown although it was still the Pope who made provision to the benefice, provided he found the king's nomination acceptable. Once Crystal's resignation as abbot was in the hands of the Pope and Reid had received the acclaim of the monks of Kinloss (which was no doubt a forgone conclusion after Abbot Crystal had made his choice) it would require the king to nominate him and then for the Pope to make provision for his installation. It would then be possible for him to travel to Rome to receive the documents of the monastery from the Pope.

Reid was at the time a secular cleric but was granted permission to rule the monastery for six months after entering into possession and thereafter, in order to be confirmed as abbot, he must take the habit and make profession. He was also granted permission to retain the perpetual vicarage of Kirkcaldy.

Mackenzie in his 'Writers of the Scottish Nation'[2] reports that Reid "performed several embassies with great success to the popes Adrian VI, Clement VII and Paul III" but provides no definite dates for these missions. It is very unlikely that he ever visited Rome in the time of Adrian VI who was pope for little more than a year at a time when Reid was subdean of Moray and of too lowly a status to have been entrusted with an embassy. There are no records of a visit to Paul III nor any reasons given by Mackenzie or others as to the nature of any such mission. The Vatican archives have been extensively studied for all references to Scottish affairs and such records preserved on microfilm in Glasgow University archives. There does not appear to be any mention among them of any visit by Robert Reid to the Vatican. However there is no doubt that he did visit Pope Clement VII toward the end of 1527 in connection with his provision to the monastery of Kinloss and it is known that he passed through Paris on his return from Italy.

He could scarcely have chosen a worse time to visit Rome and, indeed, may never have got that far.

iv. Visit to the Pope

Reid travelled to Italy toward the end of 1527. It was not a good year in the life of the papacy, especially that of the Pope himself. The perennial bout of rivalry between the French and the Emperor had seen Clement VII vacillating in his support between the Hapsburg emperor and Francis 1 of France, finally coming down on the side of the latter. Like many of his decisions it was the wrong one and the multinational forces of the Emperor under the renegade French constable, the duke of Bourbon, advanced on Rome in the spring of 1527. On the 6th May the attack on the city began and, after an initial set back, the ragged, unpaid and half starving forces of the emperor overcame a half-hearted resistance and entered the city desperate for plunder. From then on Rome became a place of unimaginable horror. The rioting troops set about killing, torturing and pillaging, destroying any and everything that came their way. The dead lay in heaps, unburied on the streets or floating in the river Tiber; fine buildings became rubble; churches were desecrated; great works of art were destroyed and St. Peter's used to stable horses. The pope took refuge in the Castel Sant' Angelo where he remained a prisoner. Eventually, on hearing that the troops were threatening to cut him to pieces if they did not receive their pay, he succeeded, on 7th December, in escaping, disguised as a servant and took refuge in the beautiful little hilltop city of Orvieto. It was here that he received the delegation from Henry VIII of England requesting his authority for the king's divorce from Catherine of Aragon. He was in no mood to comply.

Reid was still in Elgin on 10th November 1527 so that, if he left for Italy after that date, he would almost certainly not have arrived until the Pope had escaped to Orvieto. In any event it is likely that he would have been advised against proceeding to Rome where foreigners would have been in as much danger as the inhabitants. He cannot have been very impressed with what he saw in Orvieto. The pope, showing all the signs of his recent deprivation, old and ill, had taken refuge in 'an old palace of the bishops of the city, ruinous and decayed... the chambers all naked and unhanged and the roofs fallen down'[3]. Not until 11th February 1528 was the pope able to leave Orvieto. He did not return to Rome until October.

Robert Reid is said to have left Rome early in 1528 and, as he did not arrive back in Scotland until the late spring, it may be that he did indeed visit the city after some order had been restored there. If so he would have been presented with a sight of devastation where over 30,000 houses had been destroyed and the population reduced by half. Nevertheless it is to be hoped that during his time in Italy he was able to see some of the great artistic achievements of the Renaissance (the patronage of which is one of the few things that can be put to Clement's credit) and meet some of the many humanist scholars of the period, something that would have satisfied his artistic and intellectual inclinations. It was, however, clearly not an auspicious time for him to observe the pivotal centre of the Christian world. It would be interesting to know what impressions he received. At all events they do not appear to have in any way diminished his strong adherence to the catholic faith. It was not the worldly trappings of authority that mattered to him but the eternal and spiritual ones.

As was evident by his rise in the esteem of his contemporaries in the Scottish church, Reid was no fool. He must have been well aware of the many crises through which the papacy had been passing during the previous century. Still fresh in the memory of the church was the schism that had resulted in no less than three popes holding sway in their various courts at one time. He would have been aware of the rise of the concilary movement which aimed to remove authority from the Vatican and place it in the hands of councils of the doctors of the church. He had experienced at first hand evidence of the damage caused by the wars that resulted from the rivalry of Pope and Emperor. He would have witnessed from his own position the growing strength of nation states, demanding the right to appoint their own prelates. Above all he would have been aware of the mounting criticism of the worldly ambitions of the clergy that seemed to have little in common with the teachings of Christ. To Reid the only way to counteract the crumbling authority of the church was to remain faithful to its basic tenets and to reinforce the positive features of the practice and discipline that had served it as a sure foundation throughout the past millennium and a half. Compromise was possible only when it reinforced the universality of the church but never when it threatened its unity. Reid no doubt believed, as did many of those clergy and laymen who held out against the tide of reformation, that it was not frail man to which he owed obedience but the office that that man represented. In this way he was able to accept, though no doubt with some regret, the conditions in which he had found the Holy See.

On his return from Italy Reid passed through Paris and was there introduced by Robert Richardson, an Augustinian canon regular of Cambuskenneth, to a remarkable scholar, Giovanni Ferrerio, an Italian from Piedmont. Robert Richardson (or Richardinus as he was known) was himself a scholar of some standing and in 1530 wrote a Commentary on the Rule of St. Augustine which he dedicated to the abbot of his monastery, Alexander Myln. Myln who was the first President of the College of Justice, was, like Reid, a progressive thinker, one of that small body of senior clergy who sought reform of the church from within.

Whilst in Paris, Richardson was probably in contact with two other Augustinian canons, Thomas Cocklaw and Robert Logie. All three Augustinians were eventually to be accused of heresy but managed to escape to England and Richardson was even sent by Henry VIII to Scotland as a Protestant preacher. In Paris Ferrerio had also made the acquaintance of such scholars as Hector Boece, George Buchanan and William Gordon, later to become bishop of Aberdeen. Together Robert Reid and Giovanni Ferrerio travelled back to Scotland. The two men formed a friendship that was to bear fruit in later years.

Reid reached Dieppe just after Easter 1528 and returned to Scotland by way of London. At Kinloss he made arrangements with Thomas Crystal to take over the duties of abbot.

The bull from the Pope appointing him Abbot of Kinloss was not brought back by Reid but followed some months later. Dated 4th July 1528 it was sent from the city of Viterbo where there was a papal residence to which Clement had repaired after leaving Orvieto (Appendix 1). The Pope had stipulated that Reid might take charge of the monastery despite being still only a secular cleric, provided he assumed the habit of a monk within six months. However it was not until a year later, in July 1529, that he took his monastic vows, and only then could he style himself Abbot. It was in the Franciscan Church in Edinburgh that he received the Cistercian habit and was anointed and blessed as abbot by Gavin Dunbar, Bishop of Aberdeen. On his return to the monastery on the second of August he was received by the monks of Kinloss who admitted him to the chapter and the fathers made obeisance to him. On the sixth he celebrated solemn Mass.

Notes

1   Mark Dilworth: "*Scottish Monasteries in the Late Middle Ages*" p.12
2   George Mackenzie: "*Writers to the Scottish Nation*" p.46
3   Christopher Hibbert: "*Rome: The Biography of a City*".

2 Prime

Dextera Domini fecit virtutatem: dextera Domini exaltavit me, dextera Domini fecit virtutatem.

i. Abbot of Kinloss

On recommending Reid to the abbacy of Kinloss, the king showed that he was being true to his expressed wish to take an interest in the affairs and reform of the church. It was an interest that tended to give way to expediency in later times. However he did at least decline to take the advice of his uncle, Henry VIII, to follow that monarch's example in dealing with the monasteries.

The Abbey of Kinloss stood a little to the north-east of the town of Forres near to Findhorn Bay on the Moray Firth. The remaining ruins of the monastic buildings lie today close to the village in open farmland. In use today as a cemetery where, among others, there are the graves of many of the young airmen killed in the last war, it retains a air of restfulness and calm that the centuries have not disturbed. In Reid's day it must have offered him a peaceful retreat from the many cares of the law and the state that were thrust upon him.

What sort of a monk did this clever, ambitious young man make? Certainly no worse than some and a great deal better than many. Poverty, chastity and obedience were, and still are, the essential vows for a man entering the life of a religious. By the early sixteenth century these requirements had undergone considerable modification or been simply ignored.

Obedience was still expected and, for the most part, given to those to whom it was due. Reid would appear to have given his obedience to his metropolitan, the cardinal archbishop of St. Andrews, though probably with some reluctance on occasions. He certainly demanded obedience from his monks and was known as a strict, though fair, disciplinarian.

Poverty, even among the monks themselves, was mitigated to the extent that they often received monetary allowances, supposedly in place of their portion and they enjoyed lives which ensured them food and shelter and a degree of comfort. Their masters, abbots and priors, especially in the more prestigious monasteries, were often wealthy men from good families who brought wealth in with them to the cloister and enjoyed the income, not only from a well endowed monastery, but often from a number of other incumbencies as well. Reid, whilst abbot, had himself retained the fruits of the parish of Grantully as well as the income from the vicarage of Kirkcaldy and no doubt enjoyed some part of the inheritance from his father's estate. The really poverty stricken clergy were the poor clerks who did the actual work of the parishes for a pittance. Meanwhile the nominal incumbents enjoyed the income from that, and often a number of other benefices, as well as doing well paid work for the state or simply enjoying a life of ease.

Chastity was still expected of the monk but he got little encouragement in its observance from his superiors. Marriage was forbidden by the church whilst fornication was against the law of God. To go against the church's laws would incur punishment whilst to disobey the law of God was merely a matter of conscience (which could be resolved in the confessional). With the appointment of the king's bastards and favourites to the ranks of the higher clergy it is not surprising that celibacy was a rarity. Nor was it much regarded. The frailty of men was to be understood even in the priesthood. After all, if popes could spawn bastards and promote them to positions of influence in the church - and the memory of Alexander VI was still fresh in men's minds - then it was not surprising that those beneath them should follow suit. Later there was believed to be the possibility that the Council of Trent might come down in favour of married priests. As it was, the humble parish priest had his "housekeeper" and the bishops their concubines. Some like David Beaton and Marion Ogilvie enjoyed a stable and long-standing relationship, with their seven surviving children finding preferment in the church or making advantageous marriages. Other ecclesiastics were more promiscuous, Reid's own bishop of Moray, Patrick Hepburn, was said to have had eleven children from at least three mistresses whilst Beaton's successor as archbishop of St. Andrew's, John Hamilton, was said by Knox to have 'stole his kinsman's wife'. The chastity of Robert Reid, however, does not seem to have been questioned and in that respect he was a model priest and monk.

One of the monks at Kinloss whom Reid appears to have held in high regard was Adam Elder. Here is Elder's appreciation of Reid as a monk:[1]

"Moreover you have known how willingly (when he is allowed by serious business of his friends, and others who strike his ears and by the

30

many other occupations for which he is in want, either most rarely or never) and how modestly he does retire usually to read holy scripture, enjoying daily meditation on the Lord's sweetness and making his breast a library of Christ so as to be able to supply his sheep with the food of the word of God properly as befits a good shepherd, allowing no, or short, time to slip away in vain; he is far from wishing to spend what remains of his time in leisure for telling stories according to the custom of very many. How frequent and sweet are his delights; prayers, gospels, psalms, canticles and other of God's lectures. Many have experienced for many years already, and some for single hours, with what fatherly care and solicitude does he, as father of the needy and desolate, console and encourage the abandoned and the deserted, not only with counsel and words, but how kindly he is accustomed to assist with things and help, rightly considering that service which he renders and distributes in misfortune of others, courteously and kindly, is excellently reserved for the day of retribution. What is this but to be a true monk and religious?"

Elder, like others of his contemporaries, lays emphasis on Reid's love of books:

"He did not esteem riches as highly as the beloved libraries supplied abundantly with books, each most exquisite."

He goes on to reveal his abbot's opposition to the opinions of the reformers and his work in the restoration and beautifying of church buildings:

"Moreover it is well known how keenly he gives zealous aid to evert, dissipate and utterly extinguish the condemned opinions, the sects cut by the Church of Christ, the labyrinth of useless investigations which we see raging everywhere in these turbulent and exasperating times. How he does not allow these novelties to break out independently, to spread about any longer, to take vigour any more, to strike roots any deeper; it is not necessary at all to enumerate things greater than these, namely churches to the honour of the saints partly erected by him from foundation and partly made more majestic with structures and magnificent pictures; for these are not hidden in situation in darkness but are visible and exposed to light."

Elder's Latin, we are told, is exquisite but inevitably loses something in translation! Nevertheless, although the preacher is obviously at pains to make the most of all Reid's achievements, the records do bear out his description of the abbot as builder and beautifier and there is no reason to doubt his sincerity in other respects. If Reid's views regarding the protestant reformers were to be tempered by the opinions of his friends in later life, it is probable that during his tenancy of the monastery of Kinloss he was as adamantly opposed to them as Elder suggests and as is reflected in Elder's sermons, which no doubt had the abbot's approval.

Elder does not mention Reid's revival of education at the monastery. No doubt this would have involved him in an appreciation of the work of Giovanni Ferrerio and he could probably not bring himself to commend the work of one whom he was to regard as an adversary. It is a pity that the abbot's tolerance could not have been displayed among his subordinates who should have been following the example that they praised so highly.

ii. Reform of monastic communities

In 1531 the king requested the Abbot-General of Citeaux, Guillaume Le Fauconnier, and members of the General Chapter of the Cistercians, to provide an abbot to visit and reform the Cistercian order in Scotland. Whether he considered Kinloss as among those monasteries requiring reformation is not known but would seem unlikely. The emissary sent from Citeaux in 1531 was Symon Postel, abbot of Chaalis, who seems to have succeeded in causing more problems than he solved.

As father abbot and immediate superior of that abbey, Reid accompanied the abbot of Chaalis to the monastery of Deer, one of the monasteries apparently in need of reform. The chief complaint of abbot Symon, in denouncing that abbey's conduct, was directed against the holding of corporate possessions by the monks, 'the damnable vice of ownership' as he called it.

The demands of the commissioner, who was clearly ignorant of conditions in Scotland, were evidently considered by Reid to be quite impracticable and also impossible to implement in the time allowed, especially in regard to the situation of the monastery at Deer. He decided therefore to relax the abbot's demands and issued his own directions for reform, whilst awaiting for further instructions from the Chapter-General at Citeaux, once Abbot Symon had returned there.

He therefore decreed the following:

"First, that the prior and the monks, with the assent of the abbot, should appoint two or more bursars whose duty it would be, to collect the money and victuals for sustenance (food, clothes etc.) and all other necessities of the brethren and of their common servants which they should, without delay, distribute where necessary to both the healthy and the sick, the travellers and the relatives of the brethren visiting casually, so that there should be no just cause for complaint; this should be done in accordance with the rules and statutes of the reformed monasteries of the order, and proper accounts kept.

Secondly, the abbot should appoint servants whose prime duty would be to serve, chiefly the brethren advanced in years and, secondarily, to apply themselves to common works in the monastery; no monk should have commensals, and only the officials may have special servants; a monk should be appointed to distribute food and necessities to those common servants, any left over to be given to the poor.

Thirdly, with the abbot's permission, gardens should be allowed within the precincts where no unlawful intercourse would be able to take place; the bursars would collect the fruits of the gardens, as already prescribed, and distribute them for the benefit of the community and for charity, with the consent of the abbot.

All monks should observe the reformed injunctions from Citeaux, when they should be issued, strictly, entirely and faithfully and, meanwhile, those of the present more relaxed regime. Furthermore, Reid ordered the celebration of the ceremonies, devotion and learning and that fuller observance of the statutes "Liber Usuum, Libellus et Novellae diffinitorum ordinarium atque ceremonarium" should be read and explained in the presence of the entire community and practiced according to the copy received from the monastery of Coupar. The whole was to be read on the 24th of the sixth month and again every year as it is enjoined in the Part VII, chapter V of the "Libellum diffinitionum" and in the "novellis". Further a chamber for the sick should be prepared and furnished with the appropriate utensils together with a heated room with sufficient number of neck-clothes. Grammar or arts shall be read to the junior brethren every weekday and to others (even those advanced in years) if fit and in need. The commensals and all secular servants of the brethren (except those whom the abbot retains as common servants) should be removed from the cloister before the thirty-first day of May and not allowed to be received and kept in the monastery again. The monks must abstain from meat on Mondays and during the whole of Lent. The abbot to direct his attention to the repair of the buildings of the monastery beginning with the choir of the church."

Thus whilst insisting on a greater degree of austerity by depriving the monks of their servants, on whom they had evidently been accustomed to rely, Reid laid emphasis on the care of the sick, the elderly and the poor. Also evident is his passion for improving the fabric of church property, something for which he was to become renowned.

With the approval of Abbot Robert, it is reported that the abbot of Deer and the monks decided to live a regular and reformed life from that time, and to have all the fruits of the monastery in common only - and a cellarer!

Having instituted all these reforms at Deer, there is little doubt that Reid ensured that similar rules were in force in his own monastery.

Whether there were any further instructions from Citeaux is not apparent. It is probable that Reid had done their work for them.

iii. Priory of Beauly

In July 1531 the commendator of the priory of Beauly, James Baudoven, who was a canon regular and not a monk, decided - or it was decided for him - that he was no longer able to administer the priory. Whether he felt that he was unfit for the job or wished for a quieter life, he asked to be given a secular benefit in place of the cares of a priory. Beauly was a Valliscaulian foundation, only three of which had been established in Scotland. In 1510 Beauly was said to have been transferred to the Cistercians, although the monks seem to have retained the habit of the Valliscaulians. The king therefore decided it would be appropriate for a Cistercian prior to take charge and provide the necessary religious supervision. The obvious choice was the abbot of Kinloss since Kinloss is situated on the Moray Firth and Beauly at the head of the Beauly Firth. They lie about thirty miles apart and, although travel over land would have been comparatively easy, by water it would have been even simpler, indeed Reid may well have travelled by the long boat of 24 oars that he had had made to carry stones and timber for the building works at the abbey.

The Priory of Beauly stood at the entrance to the highlands. The remains of the priory church are still a prominent feature of the little town of Beauly and, like the ruins of Kinloss, retain an air of peace and sanctity.

The prior would almost certainly have had contact with the neighbouring highland clansmen. Reid is known to have had friendly relations with the Frasers and no doubt other highland families looked to Beauly for spiritual guidance. The education of the young members of local families were also the concern of the new prior.

The king had proposed that the two men swap benefices and it was agreed that Reid should become prior of Beauly and Baudoven obtain the vicarage of Grantully of which benefice Reid had retained the fruits. Adam Muir, who had become perpetual vicar of the united churches of Grantully and Drumdelgy on Reid's elevation to the abbacy, agreed to resign them in favour of James Baudoven (one wonders whether he had any choice) and, in addition, Reid agreed an annual pension for James from the fruits of the priory. The pope, Clement VII, was asked to approve the arrangements, which he duly did, so Reid added the commendam of Beauly to the abbacy of Kinloss whilst retaining the vicarage of Kirkcaldy and the fruits of the subdeanery of Moray (Appendix 1). At the age of thirty-five Robert Reid was fast becoming a power in the church and, like so many of his contemporaries, a pluralist holding several lucrative benefices. It is doubtful if Reid felt any particular qualms at his situation, pluralists were all too common in the ranks of the senior clergy. It was one of the abuses that were to bring down upon them the wrath of the reformers. Nevertheless he was able to carry out the duties of abbot and prior at Kinloss and Beauly with skill and determination and to bring those qualities to the many other duties that he was later to be called upon to perform.

At Beauly as at Kinloss, Reid did his best to swell the numbers of novices and improve their condition. In 1537 to the two he had already taken into profession of the Valliscaulian order at Beauly, he added another five and sent one of his monks from Kinloss, John Person, to instruct them. At the same time he arranged for young men from families in the neighbourhood to be educated at Beauly. These included Alexander, the second son of Hugh Fraser, Lord Lovat, and his heir. Reid took a personal interest in the education of the young Alexander Fraser and, despite occasional differences, a close bond grew up between them.

In 1541, the year in which Reid was made Bishop of Orkney, on his return from the islands, he took five of the junior monks from Beauly to Kinloss so that they might have the benefit of learning from Ferrerius. They are named as Thomas Togny, David Dason, John Crawford, James Pont and Gilbert Gray.

iv. Reid as builder

Wherever he went Robert Reid left his mark as a renovator and builder. In 1537 he began on the monastic buildings of Kinloss. In that and the following year he erected three arches in the corners of the cloister; built a new pyramid shaped dovecot or pigeon-house near to the mill; a kiln and a spacious house nearby in which to prepare malt and two large barns for storing grain; he raised the already magnificent abbot's dwelling and added vaults to the basement and restored the hall. The abbot's house was built in the form of a round tower, the ruins of which can still be seen at Kinloss. Reid obviously favoured such an architectural form since he was to build a round tower for his dwelling in the bishop's palace in Kirkwall, the ruins of which are still a landmark in the town. His most notable addition to the buildings at Kinloss was probably the spacious fire-proof library for which he provided many of the books to add to the already extensive collection made by his predecessor Abbot Thomas Crystal. The church roof he covered with lead. It was for the purpose of bringing timber and stones for the buildings that he commissioned the long boat of twenty-four oars. Whether this was the same boat that he used for travel between Kinloss and Beauly or whether he had special pleasure barge made for the purpose, as has been suggested, is uncertain.

Thomas Crystal, Reid's predecessor, had built a house for himself, Abbotshall, near Ellon, which has been wrongly ascribed to Reid himself. It is possible that, with his passion for improvement, Reid enlarged and renovated Crystal's house. His principal dwelling, however, was surely the house he had built at Kinloss.

It was at this time, when the work was completed, that he brought a distinguished painter, Andrew Bairham, to Kinloss to decorate the new buildings. Bairham was a cripple, lame in both legs. During the next three years he adorned the chapels, in the church of Kinloss, of St. Magdalene, St. John the Evangelist and St. Thomas of Canterbury, with fine paintings on panels. He also decorated the abbot's chamber and oratory, and an adjoining larger room, in a lighter style fashionable at the time, no doubt affording the abbot a rather more elegant and civilised milieu than that enjoyed by his monks. All of which adds to the picture of Reid as a man of the renaissance in whom the appreciation of beauty in no way detracted from his strict moral and religious character.

During his journeys to France for his king, Reid may well have passed though the French port of Dieppe a number of times. No doubt it was on one or more occasions that he made the acquaintance of a discharged French naval rating from that town who had lost one of his feet in action against the Spaniard. This man, Guilliaume Lubias, had acquired the experience, during his service, of treating wounds. Since his discharge he had taken up employment as a gardener. His proficiency in growing and grafting fruit trees had become well known. Reid saw the opportunity of improving the gardens at Kinloss and engaged Lubias to serve the monastery. Not only did he do so with success but was also in much demand throughout Moray for his skill both as a gardener and for treating the injured.

At Beauly, Reid had stone prepared for the nave of the church which was completed, after he became bishop of Orkney, and roofed with oaken tiles. In January of 1541 the bell tower at Beauly was destroyed in a storm either by being blown down or struck by lightening. Reid was responsible for its repair. After having been made bishop, Reid remained commendator of Beauly and in 1544 he again returned to Beauly with more plans for rebuilding. He saw to the pulling down of the old dilapidated priory buildings and their replacement by a spacious and handsome house with six vaulted rooms on the ground floor described in the Book of Kinloss as "a palace and principal building of the messuage in the place of the Priory of Beauly erected by the late Robert, Bishop of Orkney and prior of the said monastery, on the east side of the church of Beauly". It is probable that Lubias was employed in the garden of the renovated priory as well as at Kinloss and evidence of his work perhaps remained in an ancient apple and a pear tree still present in 1873 (the pear a jargonelle and the apple 6 feet in circumference according to Batten in his 'Historical Notes of the Priory of Beauly')[2].

The priory was to become the property of Lord Lovat after the Reformation.

v. Ferrerius

Giovanni Ferrerio was born, in 1502 on the Feast of the annunciation, in the small town of Rippa-near-Chieri in Piedmont in the area of Northern Italy known to the Romans as Insubria (Cisalpine Gaul) at the foot of the Alps. He tells us that his father was Martino Ferrerio and his mother Katherina Finella. His paternal grandfather, Gulielmo Ferrerio, was a consular and a man of honour, who lived until he was 103 (according to his grandson's account!); his paternal great-grandfather, Martino, a vigorous military leader and an outstanding constable; and his paternal great-great-grandfather, Tommaso, a consular and doctor of canon and civil law.

Giovanni was educated first in Chieri then in Turin where he studied the humanities. In 1525 at the age of twenty-three he went to Paris and there he studied theology at the College of Luxeuil-les-Bains under Master Morand.

It was in Paris, in 1528, that he first met Robert Reid, who was returning from Rome, and travelled with him to Scotland. On his arrival there he went, first of all, to the Scottish court where he remained for three years. There he enjoyed the company of a circle of friends one of whom, Walter Mallen, was the abbot of Glenluce, a Cistercian house with a turbulent history.

Whilst Ferrerio was with the court in Perth, the Franciscans, keen astronomers, reported a new phenomenon in the sky of unusual size whose rays were like a "field of burning reeds". The king, worried at the possible significance of the phenomenon, sought the advice of astrologers. Ferrerio however produced a treatise rejecting such a course and advised the king that, instead of depending on astrological signs and wonders, he should seek "his only hope, not in the stars, but in what is above the stars, that is, in the saints of God, particularly in our most merciful Lord Jesus". At the same time, anxious not to offend the Franciscans he praised them as "men both good and holy".

He also became acquainted during this time with the old abbot of Kinloss, Thomas Crystal, whom he came to admire. It may have been partly on Abbot Thomas' recommendation that Ferrerio accepted Reid's invitation to join him at Kinloss, which he did in 1531. At Kinloss he was to write that "he spent the next five years in monastic duties, or in my own private study or in publishing a number of new commentaries." In fact much of his time was spent in lecturing to the monks. The abbey of Kinloss under his tutelage took on some of the aspects of a university. He also had contact with an actual university at Aberdeen and expressed admiration for several of its scholars, William Hay, Alexander Galloway, Robert Gray and John Vaus and above all Hector Boece, the historian, whom he had already got to know in Paris. He also sent students from Kinloss to the University at Aberdeen. Although he taught only in Latin and in neither Hebrew nor Greek, yet the authors he expounded ranged widely from Aristotle and Virgil to contemporary writers several of whom were influential on the reformers.

The treatises on which he lectured were as follows:

From Aristotle - Ethics, Politics and Economics and on the Heavens, the Universe and Prophesying; from Cicero - de Officiis, de Amicitia, de

Senectute, Paradoxa, Somnium Scipionis, his speech pro Milone; from C. Cornel - Carnificius (or Cicero) Rhetorica ad Herennium; from John Holywood (Sacrobosco) - de shraera mundi; from Jaques Lefevre (Faber Stapulensis) – dialogi ad physicorum intelligentiam introductorii, his commentary on Aristotle's Physics and on Aristotle's On Soul, introductio in metaphysicorum libros Aristotelis and Dialogi ad metaphysicorum intelligentiam introductorii and the commentaries on Aristotle's On the heavens and On the Universe. Of more recent authors he lectured on Melanchton's Syntax; Peter Lombard's commentary on Psalm 1, Sententiarum liber IV; George of Trebizon's Dialectic; Peter Rossetus' the poet "Paulus"; Erasmus' commentarii de duplici copia and of the Latin authors, Virgil's Bucolics and the Aeneid; M. Fabius Quintilianus' de institutione oratoria; Terence's Andria; Rudolph Agricola's de Inventione dialectica; Dionysius (Pseudo-Areopagite)'s Celestial Hierarchy, of the Ecclestiastical Hierarchy, on the Divine Names, of Mystical Divinity. Other works on which Ferrerio lectured which are unknown today: Introductiones or Tabellae in logicen and parva logicalia by Lefevre, with Ferrerio's own commentary and Institutiones rhetoricae and de figuris by Melanchton and praecepta elegantarium by Agostino da Sienna).

It is interesting to see the works of Melanchthon included since Philip Melanchthon, professor of Greek at Wittenburg, was a close disciple of Martin Luther. He had however a more ecumenical outlook than most of the reformers. It is said that many of his works were even read by members of the papal curia. Erasmus, the leading humanist of his day, would undoubtedly have been closely studied by both Ferrerio and Reid.

Ferrerio was a relative of Stefano, Bishop of Vercelli who was a patron of the Lefevre group. Jacques Lefevre d'Etaples, with Guillaume Farel, created cells of reforming studies that embodied some of Luther's ideas, such as the bible should be available to all who wished to read it. Lefevre had himself produced a French vernacular version of the Bible. Some of the members of the group even preached against the selling of masses, purgatory and the cult of the saints. Lefevre had also been the teacher of Josse Clichtove, probably the most illustrious Parisian doctor of theology of the sixteenth century and an ardent, though conservative, reformer. It is evident that both Ferrerio and Reid were influenced by these and other humanist philosophers of the day. It is doubtful however whether Ferrerio or Reid would have been sympathetic to the teachings of many of the other protestant theologians writing at the time.

In the library at Kinloss, which Reid built to house the collection of books that abbot Crystal had made, were many volumes furnished by Reid and Ferrerio which give evidence of their catholic and humanist tastes. (see Appendix 2.)

The treatises on which Ferrerio taught were both read in chapter, as though lecturing a body of students; and privately to small groups of monks, as at a tutorial. James Pont and John Cameron (Capronius) are two of those who are mentioned as having received individual tuition.

He also taught the monks at Beauly and corresponded with the subprior of Deer, the monastic house under the supervision of the abbot of Kinloss.

Ferrerio, arriving at Kinloss in 1531, remained there five years. He undoubtedly had great influence on both the abbot and the monks. Ferrerio and Reid, with their humanists sympathies, were in advance of most of their catholic contemporaries, however conservative their views might appear to us to-day.

During his time at Kinloss, Ferrerio wrote a history of the monastery. Before starting it he asked his abbot to obtain information from the abbeys of Melrose, Culross and Coupar Angus regarding the monks that had come to Kinloss from those monasteries. When the work was finished he dedicated it to Robert, abbot of Kinloss. Like much of pre-Reformation history, the accuracy of much of Ferrerio's Historia however has since been called in question.

In 1537, disgusted at the advances the reformers were making among the Scots, Ferrerio returned to Italy but in 1540 he was in Paris on his way back to Scotland once more.

From Paris Ferrerio wrote to Reid. The letter formed an introduction to a commentary he had written on a work by the fifteenth century Italian scholar Pico della Mirandola. Pico was a brilliant polymath with a reputation as a scientist who produced countless propositions and became interested in the kabballa, a form of Jewish mysticism, which he endeavoured to relate to Christian teaching. He developed a pantheistic vision of creation and refused to accept the doctrine of the Trinity. He became a follower of Savanarola, the Dominican friar whose preaching had roused the citizens of Florence to throw out the Medici and return to a life of austerity and pure living. (The Dominican's criticism of the scandalous conduct and corruption of the papal court led to his excommunication by Pope Alexander VI and eventually to his rejection by the people of Florence where he was tortured, hanged and burned).

Ferrerio, a child of the Renaissance, was, like many humanist scholars of the time, greatly influenced by the works of the ancient Greek philosophers and especially Aristotle whose works many believed foreshadowed much of the Christian ethic. Of Pico's treatise he writes : "Not only is the author someone who has produced the most holy and most learned work of any of his contemporaries in Italy, but his own capacities render him suitable for the task of examining Aristotle's opinion on the soul while, at the same time, scattering the darkness of certain people who are poor philosophers, a darkness which is constantly being worn away by the efforts of individuals. For everything else, for which these people are commonly accustomed to profess admiration, is absent from their own intellectual judgement, as much as we see light and darkness, death and life, differ from each other."[3] Reid, as much a humanist as Ferrerio, would certainly have agreed with these sentiments regarding the preachers of protestant doctrine. Despite all his seemingly heretical opinions and obscure theories, Pico was, like Reid and Ferrerio, only anxious to see the catholic church reborn in the light of modern scientific knowledge.

On Ferrerio's return to Scotland, in 1540, Reid, by then bishop of Orkney, suggested to Ferrerio that he should dedicate the work he had earlier written opposing the astrology of the Franciscans, to Cardinal Beaton and thereby gain the cardinal's favour. Ferrerio took his advice and, in the dedication, he advised the cardinal, that scourge of heretics, that the best way to overcome heresy and internal strife was the "love of true holiness". The Cardinal's response was clearly favourable since he gave Ferrerio responsibility for the education of his nephews, including James, the future Archbishop of Glasgow, whilst they were in Paris. After his return to Scotland Ferrerio went back to teaching at Kinloss and remained in Scotland for a further five years maintaining his contact with Aberdeen University. One of the students to whom he had given tutorials at Kinloss, John Cameron, is known to have borrowed works from that university's library.

Ferrerio again took up the post of lecturer to the monks. Reid now granted him an annual stipend of £40, an outlay for his servant and two horses.

Reid, now a bishop, was still Commendator of Beauly in 1541 when he transferred the five monks from the priory to Kinloss, where he entrusted their education to Ferrerio for the next three years. To the five monks Ferrerio expounded on the same books on which he had lectured the monks ten years previously as well as on new treatises, including Erasmus' work on 'Plenty', 'Commentarii de copia'; Cicero's speech 'pro Quinto Ligario', Topica (ad C. Trebatium); Virgil's 'Georgics', Aristotle's Physics, Organumseu libri ad logicum attinentes with Porphyry's communium 5 vocum sive Praedicabilium liber; Peter Lombard's Sententiarum liber I; St. Paul's Epistle to the Romans and St. Augustine's de Ciritate Dei. He also lectured on the Rhetorics of Melanchton the most mild of the reformers and continued to teach classics and philosophy on Renaissance and medieval lines as before.

vi. Giovanni Ferrerio and Adam Elder

In 1544 Ferrerio left Scotland for the last time. Before he left, Reid, who was about to depart on a visit to his diocese, told him that he should not only take his own books with him but was welcome to any of Reid's that he wished to have. However Ferrerio refused the offer and took only a few of his own books leaving those he no longer wanted to the library at Kinloss.

All was not peace and light in the community, however, despite the firm hand of the abbot. It would be unreasonable to suppose that even in a religious house there would not appear from time to time clashes of personality among the members. Kinloss was no exception and it is apparent that Ferrerio came into conflict with at least one of the monks. In his Historia Ferrerio tells of his patron, Robert Reid, receiving two monks soon after his appointment, Thomas Broun, who later became a superior, and James Burt, "a youth quite apt in letters". Both were handed over to Ferrerio's charge and he had not "hesitated to inflame them to good letters and universal philosophy". He also tells of Reid receiving "an excellent young man, Adam Elder, already a Master of Arts from Paris and with him a boy of good character, John Capronius, well learned in humane letters. How much each owes to my instruction and impartial admonitions, they will say better than I"[4].

His opinion of Adam Elder was to undergo considerable modification however.

It may have been a matter of jealousy on the part of both of them for Adam Elder was a monk clearly in favour with the abbot. It was to Elder that the abbot gave the office of instructor of novices and to whom he was to entrust the care and tutelage of his nephew, Walter, when the latter went to Paris to study.

Robert Reid, as abbot, attracted to his monastery men of character and ability. Two of the most outstanding were these two, Giovanni Ferrerio, the principal teacher and the monk Adam Elder, who became the principal preacher. They would seem to have had little in common with one another. Ferrerio, whilst a staunch adherent to the catholic church, was prepared to take account of the views of some of the reforming scholars, Elder had nothing but contempt and scorn for the reformers condemning them all as 'most faithful servants of the devil'. It is perhaps a tribute to Robert Reid's stature that these two men both held their abbot in such high regard. They have both left memorials to the character of Reid that are unstinting in their praise. Of course account must be taken of their possibly feeling it incumbent upon them to praise their superior, but much of what they wrote was written after Reid's departure to Orkney or even after his death.

Some of Elder's sermons are to be found in a rare book of which there are perhaps only two copies extant. Their tone is often extreme in its condemnation of the protestant reformers, reflecting the very real fear of heresy, which may also have been Reid's fear, since presumably he sanctioned the sermons. Although one would like to think that an educated and cultured cleric like Reid would himself have avoided the vituperation of Elder's utterances, such intemperate language was in use by the protagonists on both sides of the argument and, in those days, was common currency among even the most elevated of them.

Examples of Elder's style can be seen in his sermons on the Feasts of Corpus Christi and on the Immaculate Conception (three centuries before Pius IX gave the doctrine papal sanction!), among others.[5]

In the former he said: "...the most impious deserters of the catholic faith... who in our times vomit forth the blasphemies not only at the praises of the saints wickedly and increasingly but also blab the worst abominations with horrible impiety against the mystery and revered majesty of Eucharist (which the heresiarch, Luther, calls consecrated cake and the sacrifice of Mass calls idolatry)... There is one real friend of the whole race - Christ... Who is so obdurate, ungrateful and not to embrace the friend by whose labour he is liberated, unless it is a condemned Lutheran, Zwinglian, or a deplorable Calvinist? ... The greatest friend - Christ - about to go from this world left a gage of immense love - His Body and Blood... under the species of bread and wine which to this day is dedicated, incorporated into Christ... even if the impious Luther had not blushed with shame to say that the feast of the Body was invented by

Satan; and not only this did the filthy mouth of Luther dare but... condemned the indulgences of the Roman Pontiff, abolished purgatory, puffed out the free will, drove out the hierarchy of the Church... put his mouth in heaven and denied that the saints were there and maintained impudently that their merits and intercessions were of no importance. With abominable blasphemies he also assaulted Christ's mother... brought private masses into contempt, then made also solemn masses abominable, and lastly became so impious and mad that he obstinately denied that Christ should be adored in the Host." After much more of the same, the preacher urges his listeners "let us worship Christ in the Eucharist and keep the day however the synagogue of Satan devoted to Satan in satanic way contradicts and barks and let us say with Bernard: learn O christians how much you must love Christ who gave His flesh as food, His blood as drink, the soul as reward and the water of His side as laver."

On the 'Immaculate Conception' the preacher has less to say about the 'impious deserters of the catholic faith' and relies on scriptural authority to claim that the mother of Jesus was conceived without sin, in contrast to many other righteous women in scripture who were born in sin though they achieved virtue through the grace of God in life. It was a doctrine unacceptable to many of the fathers of the church such as Thomas Aquinas but, no doubt, its acceptance by the twelfth century Scottish theologian, Duns Scotus, would have had greater influence in a Scottish community. In a sermon on the feast of St. Peter and St. Paul the preacher returns to his condemnation of the reformers, 'the babblers of insane brains' and 'convulsed by the solidity of apostolic rock, let us believe what the doctors, councils believed' and again on 'Purification' the Reformers are called 'heretics with condemned minds brought together by the bewitchment of the recent doctrine'.

How much did the words of these sermons reflect the views of the abbot? Presumably quite a lot. Although anxious for reform of the catholic church and conversant with the works of such reform minded scholars as Erasmus, Reid, nevertheless, had little time for those protestants who wished to undermine the whole basis of catholic doctrine. It may be that with maturity, as he watched he advance of the protestant movement in Scotland, he may have sensed that he and his kind were facing a losing battle but, during his time at Kinloss, Scotland must still have seemed a strong bastion against the tide of reform sweeping continental Europe.

Despite the strong views expressed by Elder in his sermons, he seems to have failed in his allotted task of educating Reid's nephew, Walter, in adherence to the faith, as was to become apparent after Reid's death.

As to Elder's opinion of his abbot he expresses it by saying: "lest you suppose... that I wish to flatter you with these words spoken from this pulpit appointed for sacred discourse... do know that... at least in this entire company I see nobody that being put on oath would not first subscribe to my same words (I think I can holily swear so much)..." and he goes on to praise Reid with the words: "We all know that he is precipitate on no occasion, never rash, that he does not do or say anything but with dignity and highest praise (such is his integrity and kindness). With what wisdom, what sedulity and what care does he always give attention to extirpating vices, if perhaps they shoot forth in the flock committed to him. What a diligence does the man born for virtue apply to sowing, increasing and raising virtues everywhere, not to mention those things which belong to much more important affairs than those which may or should be inserted by me into, or fitted for, a capitular sermon. It is not necessary indeed to relate many other charitable works in which his beneficence is engaged, as pious alleviation of the poor, overwhelmed by not eating and simultaneously by years, with material sustenance; as giving in decent marriage girls whose possessions are too scanty to enable them to pay their dowry; as liberal support of many promising youths of noble birth in studying letters; as tenacious maintaining of his ardent love and eagerness for literary work which he embraced even from the beginning and when still of tender age, as display of great liberality for the lovers of good letters and for those who made them their profession; and many other things which it would be too long to relate".

Ferrerio is somewhat briefer but no less laudatory in calling Reid a "man of singular goodness, of full kindness and perfect service to the country and of dutifulness to the people and that his wisdom and vigilance is such that at home and outside that hardly could be found in anybody else in Scotland."

It was after his return to Paris, that Ferrerio wrote the commentary on Pico della Mirandola's essay on 'Immortality' which he dedicated to his patron, Robert Reid.

In 1555 he wrote to Reid from Paris recommending the Greek scholar, Edward Henryson, and it was probably through Reid's patronage that Henryson was appointed in the following year to give public lectures in Greek in Edinburgh. It was also at this time that Ferrerio edited and added to Boece' 'History of Scotland', possibly contributing to that work's fictional character!

Giovanni Ferrerio, scholar, theologian and humanist was undoubtedly a great influence in the life of Robert Reid who found in him a kindred soul. Both were eager to reform their church but bitterly opposed to others who sought its reformation in the destruction of the very principles and traditions upon which their faith was grounded.

Controversy arose over Ferrerio's books prior to his final departure from Scotland in 1544. When the five monks from Beauly returned to their priory, Ferrerio presented each of them with a few volumes. One of the books, "Lives of Plutarch", which he had promised to Thomas Togny, was at the time in the possession of Adam Elder. Elder not only refused to part with the book but claimed that Ferrerio possessed no books of his own and that all those he claimed had been purchased with the Abbot's money. Since, in any case, Reid had offered Ferrerio any of his own books that he should wish to take, Elder was clearly in the wrong. Ferrerio then wrote to Togny:[6]

"I am not much astonished at what you write of Adam Elder. I thought, however, that in these days when he drinks milk and water, he would not make himself such a fool; But he goes on, I see, always like himself. The argument by which he defends himself against giving up my books is of a similar stamp to the man himself - weak in the loins - for it does not necessarily follow that books belong to another although his name be written in them; just as you and your colleagues, for nearly three years, wore the cowl of the Cistercian order when you were of a different profession (i.e. Valliscaulian); for a good part of the books have the name of Abbot Thomas affixed to them by Sir James Pont when they really belonged to Abbot Robert. Besides, it is untrue that all the books were acquired with the abbot's money for, before I ever knew the abbot, I had many books in Paris and brought more with me on first coming to Scotland than the abbot himself. Then, while engaged at court, I bought not a few books in Edinburgh with my own money; and, what I procured at Paris during the last few years, many at Kinloss can attest who saw those that I brought with me at my second coming; and, if all is taken into account, you may conclude that almost half of the books were bought with my money. Is not the money my own, which I had before I came to know the abbot? or which I afterwards acquired through my own industry? More truly mine than what Adam diverts to his own use, without leave of the abbot, by selling cabbages from his garden. I indeed am of no profession (Ferrerio was never a monk) but that of Christ and what my industry brings to me is my own; but, what a monk acquires, is not for himself but for his monastery.

That I have frequently put the name of the abbot on the books arises from the love which I bear him, as though I wished all things belonging to friends to be held in common. But I ask you with what front, with what face, does Adam daily approach the altar in such manifest and perverse falsehood? May Christ grant that hereafter he may judge more candidly of our affairs; and in the mean time take care, through your sub-prior, again to claim the Plutarch which, at your departure, I, with good title, bestowed upon you."

Thomas Hastie, the sub-prior referred to, was himself not averse to engaging in dispute. In 1543 he had found himself in court to answer a charge of assaulting Gavin Dunbar, the treasurer of Ross, when in the company of his bishop and others, in the cathedral. We are not told of the cause of the quarrel nor of its final outcome but, in an age when the servants of archbishops can come to blows in the cathedral of Glasgow, such behaviour cannot be regarded as altogether exceptional!

In the letter, already referred to, that Ferrerio wrote to Reid from Paris dedicating Pico's work on Immortality to the bishop he is evidently referring to Elder when he writes; "…while I was thinking of this, I was held up by a man who, because he always wants to appear attentive, actually takes advantage of your mildness and my ingenuousness in the care of our affairs". It is a sad reflection on the Christian charity of two such presumably devout men that they should have behaved in this way toward one another and that Reid seems to have been unaware of their mutual hostility or unable to restrain it.

It is evident from his employment of Ferrerio as instructor in theology to his monks that the abbot of Kinloss was keen, not only on increasing the number of postulants to his order, but in their being thoroughly well educated. In addition to the monks he took great interest in the education of the young in general and his relatives in particular. His nephew, John Bad, a portioner of Arbirlot, a parish just west of Arbroath, he kept at school at his own expense. In a court action on 14th and 31st July 1535, Reid had helped John Bad recover the lands and fishing rights he had inherited and which he then agreed not to let out without the abbot's express consent. On the 27th of the same month, the Privy Seal Register reports a protection being granted to William, bishop of Aberdeen, his kinsmen, fiends and servants, one of whom was John Bad.

The abbot is credited with having kept a number of local noblemen's children with him for "table, lodging, conference and advice". These included the sons of Lord Lovat, Mackenzie of Kintail, Munro of Fulis and Ross of Balnagown, either at Kinloss or more probably at Beauly to where Reid had sent one of his monks, John Person, to instruct the novices.

vii. Fishing rights in the Findhorn

Churchmen in the sixteenth century were a litigious lot. It was not long after being consecrated as abbot that Reid found himself involved in law suits. It is quite possible that he enjoyed the challenges involved for he became, in time, a formidable advocate in the courts and an astute judge. Soon after settling in at Kinloss he renewed a dispute with the inhabitants of Forres which his predecessor had allowed to lapse and won for the monastery two 'baits' (pastures in which skins were steeped).

In May 1538 Reid was again required to defend the rights of his own monastery when he became the object of litigation against himself and the monastery of Kinloss.

The abbey of Kinloss lay only a few miles from the town of Forres. Close by ran the river Findhorn on its way to the Moray Firth. The fishing rights on the river were important both to the town and to the monastery of Kinloss nearby. The river would have been the source of provision to both, and to the monks especially on days of abstinence.

The king ordered the chancellor to assign a day for hearing the evidence regarding the fishing rights in the river Findhorn. It was alleged by Alexander Dunbar of Cumnok, that the abbot of Kinloss, his monastery and the town of Forres and others had wrongly withheld these rights. The abbot was required to appear at St. Andrew's to answer the charge and produce evidence of his rights. However he refused, maintaining that the monastery was being pursued by Dunbar as procurator of the town of Forres. Dunbar for his part maintained that he was at the bar to defend the privilege of that town. The abbot appealed to the king, and the lords decided that the precept of sasine of the fishing, given by Reid's predecessor to Robert Dunbar of Cumnok, should be annulled as it did not have the consent of the present abbot.

Clearly Robert Reid, the lawyer, was not a man to be lightly challenged in the courts.

The following year, in an attempt to clarify the situation further, Reid summoned Alexander Dunbar of Cumnok on three charges over the Findhorn fishing rights. It was agreed to settle the dispute by a contract on the following conditions:

1) In respect of non entries of fishing called "the common stell" in the river Findhorn during four years, Dunbar to pay £80 to the abbot for non entries and the abbot to discharge until Alexander Dunbar makes a notable fault. 2) In respect of wrong occupation of the fishing called "the post" in the mouth of the Findhorn with the part of the "common stell" and with "Feithnett" in the fresh water of Findhorn - as the abbot maintained that the fishing "northmost post" was occupied later and the fishing of southmost was part of the patrimony of the abbey in virtue of infeftment by the king, and in which Alexander alleged that his ancestors used to pay for the fishing of Feithnett to the king's controller - Alexander to take Feithnett in feufarm for 46/8 yearly, the abbot to give the precept of sasine of "common stell" to Alexander as heir to his father James. 3) Concerning the profits and duties of the part of land of west Grange contiguous to the burn of Moffat, for twenty-six years damaged through stopping in building a mill - the abbot to discharge Dunbar of profits and Alexander to renounce his right to that debatable piece of land; both parties to live in friendship.

Thus Abbot Robert judicially compelled Alexander Dunbar, the sheriff of Moray, to accept the feu of the fishing of salmon from him on new conditions. There remained settlement to be made with the inhabitants of Forres. Final accord and extinction of the suit was made before the lords of council regarding the profits of 7/16 of the fishing in the fresh water of Findhorn and other fishings violently occupied by the community of the burgh of Forres for the past five years. The lords decreed that the community should desist from occupation, renounce "the Outwater stell and the Cruikis stell" in the fishing in fresh and salt water of the Findhorn and that abbot Robert should set in feufarm to the community 7/16 of the fishing of Findhorn, a "fische net" in the fresh water, the fishing of Aithistell and 3/4 of the fishing of Elvinstell on the west side of the Findhorn as it had been occupied by the town for the last twenty years, provided that it was not lawful for the abbot to exceed two skiffs. The burgh would pay the monastery £10 as blench farm. The agreement was concluded at the end of December 1539 and the abbot would appear to have succeeded in achieving all that he set out to obtain for his monastery, although it is difficult today to follow the intricacies of a dispute couched in such medieval legal terminology.

This was not the first time that Abbot Robert had had to defend the rights of his monastery. In June of 1530 he had taken his seat as a lord of council for the first time. Shortly afterwards the procurators of the Abbot of Arbroath made an extrajudicial appeal to the pope, the archbishop of St. Andrew's and the conservator of the privileges of the monastery of Arbroath (the abbot of Dunfermline) against the Bishop of Moray and his official, which office was still held by Robert Reid. The appeal which the bishop and his official had to respond to was for having sequestrated the fruits of the churches of Aberchirder and Inverness, which belonged to the monastery of Arbroath. The bishop and his official claimed that the monastery of Arbroath had failed to pay tax due to the bishop. The abbot of Arbroath, with whom they were in dispute, was David Beaton who was later to become Cardinal Archbishop of St. Andrew's and Reid's metropolitan. The careers of both men followed somewhat similar courses and they were often to be associated in both judicial and diplomatic affairs, although, in future, on the same side. Although unlikely to have become close friends, they probably enjoyed a strong degree of mutual respect. Beaton was, of course, the more prominent of the two. Whilst both men were at the forefront of the battle against heresy and the maintenance of the catholic faith in Scotland, Beaton's aims were largely to maintain and enhance the political role of the church whilst Reid was more closely concerned with its theology.

Soon after this encounter Reid had resigned all offices connected with the diocese of Moray. He was replaced as official by Gavin Leslie who was, in turn, succeeded by Henry Sinclair and, in 1537, by Alexander Sutherland, dean of Caithness and prebendary of Duffus. As subdean Reid was replaced by William Paterson, a canon of Moray. Reid also resigned the united vicarages of Grantully and Drumdelgy which were provided to Adam Muir whilst the fruits thereof and the regression were reserved to Reid. He retained, however, the vicarage of Kirkcaldy.

At about this time the king became dissatisfied with the indifference shown by lords in deciding civil matters, he therefore ordered that 'persons of cunning knowledge' should have a vote in session and the Abbot of Kinloss was among those, appointed.

Two actions taken by the abbot at this time have been recorded. First he dissented from the verdict in an action for trespass against the privileges of the crown by two priests who had "purchased" a vicarage in Rome which could not be provided in Scotland. Such an action being contrary to an act of Parliament. Secondly, in 1531, he is recorded as being witness of a dispute between the Bishop of Galloway and his metropolitan, the Archbishop of Glasgow, though whether he played any part in its resolution is not recorded.

Notes

1. L. Nowosilski: *"Robert Reid and his Time"* MS. p.293
2. Smyth's Chronicle *"Book of Kinloss"* app. p.97 quoted in Batten's *"Charters of the Priory of Beauly"* p.220
3. Giovanni Ferrerio. Introduction to *"R. in Christo patri Dominus Robertus Reid"* - Pico della Mirandola
4. Ferrerius *"Histroria"*
5. L. Nowosilski: Ibid p.228 ff.
6. Batten: *"Charters of the Priory of Beauly"* p.221

3 Terce

Domine viam justificationum tuarum: et exquiram eam semper.

i. Senator of the College of Justice

On the 15th September 1531 at the instance of his kinsman, the Duke of Albany, the Pope issued a bull for taxing the Scottish prelates in order to raise money for a College of Justice in Scotland. An act of Parliament giving effect to the bull was passed on 17th May 1532. The clerical hierarchy were naturally unhappy at the prospect of yet more church money going to swell the royal coffers but could hardly complain at the intended object of the tax. Nevertheless it forced many church bodies to feu lands in order to raise revenue and was yet another nail, and a substantial one, in the coffin of ecclesiastical power. Another subtle shift of power from the church into royal hands was to be the appointment of five of James' under age bastard sons to wealthy abbacies. The appointment of Robert Reid to the monastery of Kinloss and Priory of Beauly was beginning to look like a noble exception to the cynical exercise of political nepotism.

The king, at the age of twenty, now fully in charge of the government, required the bishoprics and monasteries to raise the sum of 10,000 golden ducats (£10,000 Scots) a year for the maintenance of the fourteen Senators of the new college, half of whom were to be laymen and half clerics. Over these would be the lord Chancellor and a Lord President. Other 'extraordinary lords' could be co-opted as occasion required. It is not surprising that the bishops complained at having to raise such a large sum. In the event, it was eventually whittled down to £72,000 over four years together with the income from certain benefices and a contribution promised from the crown. Even then most prelates remained in arrears. Although the college came into being in 1532 it was not until 1541 that it was finally ratified by parliament.

Robert Schanwell, who had resigned the vicarage of Kirkcaldy, was among the first clerics to be appointed to the college but, at the first meeting of the court, Robert Reid was elected a Judge and admitted by the king in place of his uncle. It could be that Robert Schanwell, with advancing years, looked for a quieter life after his long academic career and was only too happy to pass the responsibility on to his ambitious young nephew. The first President of the College was Alexander Myln, the abbot of Cambuskenneth. Reid was appointed to act as president in the absence of abbot Myln and was eventually to succeed him in the office. When acting president he was required to administer the oath and his duties included the weekly examination of witnesses. His fee for attendance at session was £133.6.4. (presumably yearly).

By 1532 Reid's status in the law was being widely recognised. He was one of two judges, along with Donald, Abbot of Fearn, appointed mandatories of Silvester Dorius, the papal chaplain and auditor of Palace causes, who was envoy to James V. The two judges were called upon to summon Robert, bishop of Ross, and Hugh Fraser to confirm the grant by the bishop of the lands of Kirktoun to Hugh's father, Thomas Fraser. The grant had originally been made in 1521 along with that of Craig and the fishing of that town, commonly called the Ess of Kilmorack, which belonged to the church of Kilmorack. However the fifth Lateran Council of Julius II had, in 1514, forbidden all kings, princes and lords from seizing any ecclesiastical property without permission of the pope. In the case of the grant to Thomas Fraser, this had not been obtained. When a papal nuncio in the person of Silvester Dorius eventually arrived in Scotland, Hugh Lord Lovat hastened to request him to give full papal approval to the transaction. A jury of eight men both laymen and priests were summoned to attend in the aisle of the Virgin Mary in the Cathedral of Ross, together with the two appellants, the Bishop of Ross and Hugh Fraser. The Nuncio's letter was presented to the two judges by Hugh Fraser and they and the jury enquired into the propriety of the grant and gave judgement. The seals of the two judges were then attached to the instrument.

The Frasers were near neighbours of Reid as Commendator of Beauly and he was to become their patron and friend and to take a great interest in the education of the young Lord Lovat.

Robert Reid was now busily occupied both as a judge, and as an auditor of accounts for many departments of state. The following are some of the many matters with which he had to deal:

In 1537 Reid was again commissioner for holding the exchequer and received the gift of ward of the lands and annual rents of William

Dumbrek of that ilk (the lands of Dumbrek were in the parish of Udny) and the gift of marriage of Thomas, William Dumbrek's son and heir. Thomas Dumbrek being the father of Katherine Dumbrek, the wife of John Reid of Aikenhead, Robert Reid's nephew.

In July of 1537, as superior of the lands of Lethnot he was in court to decide where the marches between those lands, then in feu to Patrick Cheyne of Essilmont, and the lands of Troup should be established.

For the past sixty years the abbots of Kinloss had been conducting a suit against the Ogilvies, lairds of Findlater. In November 1537 Reid took up the suit. There was controversy over the debatable lands between those of Strathisla, belonging to the monastery, and the lands of Deskford, belonging to Alexander Ogilvy of that ilk and of Findlater. After judicial enquiry before parliament and the king, Reid succeeded in recovering the ground of Strathisla occupied by Alexander Ogilvy and it was decided that Ogilvy would agree to having the process of perambulation whilst the abbot and the monastery would grant the debatable lands, called Our Lady's lands of Kinloss, to Alexander.

The following month he was arbitrating in a dispute between Alexander Innes, son and heir apparent of the laird of Innes, and James Innes, son and heir apparent of Robert Innes of Rothnakenzie.

During this year he was a royal commissioner for holding the exchequer.

In March 1538 he was again lord commissioner of parliament and judge mandatory of the grand penitentiary for confirmation of feu of lands of Cragfoid by the abbot of Balmerino to Robert Douglas of Lochleven. In the same month he audited the accounts of the master of royal works.

Acting in his capacity as papal mandatory commissioner in August 1538 Reid confirmed the grant of lands of Over Mewlistown and Sarjantland to James Dundas of Craigtown and his wife, Elizabeth Hamilton, by Walter Lindsay, preceptor of Torphichen.

These represent a few of the many law suits, mostly concerned with landed property, in which the abbot of Kinloss was required to arbitrate.

One of his first financial duties was to audit the accounts of the master of the king's works. After this he was much in demand as auditor not only for his ability but undoubtedly for his known objectivity and honesty also. The latter virtue was called upon in 1531 when he found himself having to pay £52, the final instalment of a tax due from the prelates to the king, for the armed forces. At about the same time he agreed to modify the compensation due to a victim who had suffered the loss of a hand and been in peril of death.

In 1539 he was again busy auditing accounts, first for the keeper of the privy seal, then for the comptroller and those of the lord high treasurer of Scotland. He was next appointed auditor of the accounts of the subcollector of the taxes, both old and new, granted by the prelates, if somewhat reluctantly, to the king. He also audited the accounts of the master of royal works. He again audited the latter's accounts in January 1539 and in January 1540; and those of the exchequer in July 1540 as well as the accounts of the lord high treasurer of Scotland and of the comptroller in September of that year.

Further land disputes came his way in 1539 and 1540. In February 1539 he was arbitrating between the abbot of Kilwinning and Laurence Crawford of Kilbirny and his wife, Helen Campbell, respecting the lands and teinds of Crawfield; and in February of 1540 in an action over the marches between the lands of Sauqhat belonging to Robert, master of Erskine, and of Quiltors belonging to Gilbert Gray of Sheves. In April 1540 he had been required by Anthony, the papal plenipotentiary, to confirm the grant of the lands of Adrey by Patrick, bishop of Moray, to John Grant of Ballindalloch.

In 1540 Reid attended at the condemnation of Sir John Borthwick for heresy. John was the younger son of Lord Borthwick who, like Reid's father, had been killed at Flodden. He had come under the influence of a relative, Nicholas Borthwick, who had studied at Wittenberg and, like Ferrerius and Reid himself, had come to know Robert Richardson (who was himself to be charged with heresy) whilst studying at the college of St. Victor in Paris. Borthwick was also in correspondence with Thomas Cromwell and had introduced the English ambassador, Sir Ralph Sadler, to Edinburgh. He escaped to England, was tried in absentia and sentenced to the stake. In his absence an effigy of him was burnt at St. Andrew's. After the Reformation his sentence was revoked. How Reid regarded this farce is not known.

Among other duties during 1540 Reid was "oversman" to the testament of James, earl of Moray; auditor of the exchequer, of the accounts of the lord high treasurer of Scotland and of the comptroller; arbiter on the side of Hucheon Ross of Kilravock in a case against Sir Robert Campbell about a debatable piece of land between the Mains of Calder and lands between Calder, Kilravock, Geddes and Raitt; lord commissioner of parliament on several occasions and elected a lord of the articles in December. In 1541 he was an executor for Mr. Henry White, dean of Brechin and again Lord commissioner of parliament on a number of occasions.

Whilst he undertook his judicial duties, the abbot, the monastery and its possessions were taken under royal protection. As a special favour to abbot Robert for his good services, the king created the village of Seyton of Kinloss, the principal harbour of the River Findhorn, to be free burgh of barony. Thereafter, with the abbot's consent, the burgesses were allowed to elect bailies, erect a mercat cross, keep a weekly market and feu the lands in particles, and the abbot redeemed a portion of fishing of the bait occupied by the inhabitants of Forres.

ii. Ambassador to Henry VIII

Now, in addition to his duties as a judge and the calls upon him to audit the accounts of numerous bodies, Reid was required to undertake the roll of diplomat.

Toward the end of 1533 trouble was brewing on the border, the truce of Berwick was about to expire and, on 7th January 1534, the English began an invasion of Scotland. Adam Otterburn of Auldhame was sent by James as ambassador to Henry VIII of England, initially to discuss a possible marriage between Henry's daughter Mary and the Scottish king but principally to agree a peaceful settlement and to avoid further incursions of the English over the Scottish border.

King James V to King Henry VIII:

Richt Excellent, Richt Hie, and Mychty Prince, our derrest Uncle and brother, We recommend Ws unto You in maist hertlie maner. Forsamekle as We have directit presently unto You our traist Counsalour, Maister Adam Ottirburn of Auldhame, as ane personage in quhome We have singulair traist and confidence, and als as he that hes ay bene a procurer and sollistar of peace and concord to be betuix Ws and our Realmes, to declair unto You our inwart muynd, and how desirouse We ar to have your hertly kindnes pece and rest betuix Ws and our Realmes, and thairto communicate uther thingis, that may tend to the weil tharof, lik as We have geven him in command and charge; praying You, derrest Uncle, to gif to him gud attendance and credence, as to Our self.

Richt Excellent, Richt Hie, and Mychty Prince, our derrest Uncle and Brother, God Almychty have You in keping. Gevein under our Signet at our burgh of Couper, the 22 day of Novembre, and of our Regine the twenty ane zeir.

(signed) Your loving Brother and Nepho,
James R.[1]

Otterburn seems to have had only one audience with the king who was waiting for other more prestigious ambassadors with whom to discuss peace. Henry led the ambassador to believe that Mary Tudor might be deprived of the succession to the English throne in favour of James since she was, in his view, though not that of the pope, a bastard, being the daughter of Catherine whom he claimed never to have married legitimately. Whilst in England, Otterburn also had discussions with the imperial ambassador, Chapuys.

On the 16th February James commissioned Adam Otterburn and the Bishop-treasurer of Scotland, William Stewart, bishop of Aberdeen, to travel to London to complete the agreement and wrote to Henry to inform him of their coming. Later, at the request of the bishop, Robert, abbot of Kinloss, was added to the commission.

"Richt Excellent, Richt Hie, and Mychty Prince, our derest Bruthir and Uncle, We commend Ws unto You in our maist hertlie maner. Signifiand on to You We have directit our Thesaurar, and richt weilbelovit traist counsailour, William Bischope of Abirdene, our Ambassiatour towart You, wyth all informationis and instructionis necessair for the weill of the peax betuix Ws and our Realmes; and for the experience traist and confidence We have in our traist Counsalour Robert Abbot of Kinloss, and at the desir of the forsaid Reverend Fader, hes wyth him send towart You our said Abbot and counsalour, quhome we desir You, derrest uncle, to treit in honest maner as efferis, and to admit him in cousalis and secretis quhatsumever concernyng our materis, as the said Reverend Fader, our Ambassiatour, requiris, as man luffand the weill of the peax and concord evir to stand beuix Ws and our Realmes.

Richt Excellent, Richt Hie, and Mychty Prince, our derrist Bruthir and Uncle, We pray God Almychty have You in His Keping. Gevin onder our Signet, at our castel of Stirling, the penult day of Februar, and of Regine ye tuenty ane zeir.

(signed) Your lovyng Brother and Nepho, James R. [2]

The ambassadors were to be accompanied by Sir William Ogilby of Douglas; Barclay of Cullerny; the heir of Balwearie; the lairds of Mynto and Elphinston; parson of Kilearn; Mr. Walter Buyis, parson of Snow; Robert Grey of Medytene; Mr. William Stewart, vicar of Pencaitland together with thirty or more attendants and seventy horses. During the Abbot's absence the Abbey of Kinloss and the Priory of Beauly as well as Reid's relatives were again taken under royal protection.

Reid and the others arrived at Ware in Hertfordshire on the 8th March 1534 (after a number of false starts) but did not reach London, less than a day's ride, until Monday the 23rd. Possibly these were diplomatic delays on the part of the ambassadors, or they may have been waiting further instructions from James (possibly the secret letter dated 18 March which was later to be the cause of complaint from the bishop). On the 24th they made a solemn entry into the city where they were met by the Earl of Northumberland with twenty horses - "never a goodlier embassage from Scotland was seen before" - and conducted to their lodgings in the Taylor's Hall. Two days later they dined with the council in the Star Chamber. The following day they were brought to the royal palace at Westminster to show their commission and message and pay their respects to the king and to "the lady" (the Pope having refused to countenance Henry's divorce from Catherine, the Scottish bishops could hardly acknowledge Anne as queen). In order to persuade the Scottish king to accept the legitimacy of his marriage to Anne, Henry was prepared to recognise James' claims on the succession. The date of the meeting was also the 'feast of the annunciation' and, Anne being again pregnant, it has been suggested that Henry may have thought it an appropriate day for her to be presented!

The bishop, the abbot and their party were entertained to a banquet by the Duke of Norfolk and the Privy Council at Westminster where they talked until 4.0 p.m. Later they attended a meeting of Parliament where the lords were present in their robes. Meanwhile the king discussed the question of the succession with parliament.

The Scots were then kept in suspense for over a fortnight. Eventually the king appointed Sir Thomas Audley, the chancellor; Thomas Cromwell, his first secretary; Edward Fox, the grand almoner; John Trigunwell, principal judge of admiralty and Richard Gwent, the official principal of Canterbury, to enter into discussion with the Scots over the conclusion of a peace treaty.

There was talk of a meeting between the three monarchs of England, France and Scotland. The imperial ambassador, Eustace Chapuys, thought no such meeting could take place before an agreement between the English and the Scots. Otterburn, who was on close terms with Chapuys, believed that the Scots would be better off under the protection of the catholic emperor who had no love for Henry, after his repudiation of Catherine who was the emperor's aunt. Otterburn arranged for the Bishop of Aberdeen and the Abbot of Kinloss to meet Chapuys so that he might enlighten them on imperial policy.

The emperor Charles was anxious to bring Scotland into the imperial orbit by having James marry a Hapsburg bride, either Mary, the widow of the King of Hungary, who disliked the idea, or a Danish princess. Otterburn who appeared to be conspiring against the English king, was strongly in favour of such an alliance with the catholic emperor. He believed that the agreement between Henry and Francis I of France, which Henry assured the Scots had taken place, would leave the Scots without the protection of a French alliance (The seigneur de la Pomeroy, as envoy for the French king, had arranged the meeting of the English and French monarchs). Otterburn did his best to persuade the bishop to Chapuys' point of view and even threatened to go direct to James to persuade him of the 'virtuous and catholic proposition' of the Emperor. Henry, of course, was averse to James allying himself with either the French or the imperial royal families.

The bishop and abbot Robert let Otterburn know that they thought that it would be dishonourable to solicit for peace with England whilst, at the same time, allying themselves with the emperor. Otterburn grudgingly agreed with the two clerics whilst at the same time agreeing with Chapuys that the Scots should join the emperor's forces in an attack on the English. He did however support the bishop in endeavouring to obtain a firm declaration that James should succeed to the English throne in the event of Mary Tudor dying before her father.

The bishop of Aberdeen was now anxious to conclude the peace with England but there continued to be delays, the English seeming to be in no hurry to settle the matter.

Life at the English capital however was not entirely taken up with diplomatic business. Apart from being entertained with wine and song and 'his majesty's Paramour', they were also invited to be present at the execution of a nun. In this there was no thought of intimidating the catholic ambassadors but merely with providing them with a spectacle! The nun, Dame Elizabeth Barton, had, so she claimed, been commanded by God to enter the religious life. She had been told by our Lady that she had been so confirmed in grace that she had no need of prayer, had received a golden letter from St. Mary Magdalene and that angels brought the host to her from the priests. If that were all she might have avoided prosecution. However her revelations had taken a political turn. At the command of an angel she revealed to the king that he would not remain on the throne for a month after his marriage to Anne Boleyn and would be dead after six months. She had even been given a sight of the place in hell prepared for him! She also maintained that Cardinal Wolsey had died (in 1530) fifteen years before God would have had him and that it was she who prevented Wolsey from agreeing to Henry's divorce from Catherine. She herself wrote to the pope to prevent Henry from marrying Anne and although Clement had in any case ruled against Henry it was claimed that his Holiness had been influenced in his decision by "the diabolic plot of the said nun".

She was not however without followers and even Warham, archbishop of Canterbury, was prepared to listen to her. John Fisher, bishop, of Rochester, was imprisoned for treason for not revealing what she had told him. She was later to confess, presumably under torture, that she had never had a vision in her life.

On the twentieth of April she and a number of her followers were hanged at Tyburn and their heads displayed on London Bridge and the gates of the city. Although Robert Reid may have been accustomed to the sight of heretics being burnt in his own country, he and the other Scots found it ridiculous to suppose that such executions would incline Henry's subjects to accept his defiance of the Pope. They must also have had misgivings at the sight of a catholic nun being thus publicly executed. Yet even Thomas More, a staunch English catholic and one who also deplored the king's divorce and was soon to meet a similar fate, considered her to have been a wicked woman.

When the Scots again met Henry it is said - though there are no written records to that effect - that Reid impressed the king with his shrewdness and business ability.

The bishop of Aberdeen, who was leading the delegation had an objection to make. According to Robert Lyndsay of Pitscottie in his 'Cronicles of Scotland'[3] they carried a secret letter to the king of England but 'when the bischope of Aberdeine was sett at the counsall, and seeing monie wryttingis of uther ambassadoures lying at the bord for thair awin affaires, as they had adoe in diversis realmes, he also saw the king of Scotlandis secreit wrytting lying among thame, and also soone as he perseaved it, he start up from the boord, and tuik the king by the sleive, and led him to a window, and said to him, "Sir, if I durst say with your licence, yea have failed to our maister the king of Scotland." King Harie answeired, "Quhairintill, sir bishchope, for rather or I failed willinglie to the king of Scotland, my sister sone, I had rather perrill my croun and all that I have, in on day, thairfoir tell me quhairin?" The Bischope answeired, "Ye promeist that no man sould sie the secreit letter that I brought to yow, bot your awin bodie onlie; and now it is lying patent and oppin at your boord, that ony man may reid it quha is at yon boord." The king answered and said, "Sir bischope yea are deceaved, thair is no man yonder but my awin bodie, they in me, and I in thame, nather dare they reveal any thing they sie yonder, under paine of the executioun of themselffis, and forfalting both of thame and thair posteritie; and if your king use any other meanes privilie, nor his wise counsallouris, aither in the government of his boidie, or his realme, he will not reigne long, nor have his realme in peace and rest; thairfoir, shew your maister that nather he nor I may be estemed sundrie from our counsaloweres if we wold ruell weill.""

The letter in question may have been the one written by James to Henry on the 18th March:

Richt Excellent, Richt Hie, and Mychty Prince, oure derrest Uncle and Bruthir, We recommend Ws unto Yow in oure maist hertlie maner, signifiand unto Yow that, sen oure last depesche gevin to Yow with oure Ambassiatoure and Thesaurare, hes beene maid on oure Marcheis, be evill myndit personis youre subjectis, sik invasioun and violence, as may be grete occasioun to breke this abstinence, standing betuix oure Realmez and liegijs, quhairof ane parte oure said Ambassiatoure and Thesaurare can schaw; the uthir and gretest of all attemptatis that wes done aganis oure leigijs during the hale weire, sen his departing, hes bene committit upon oure Myddill Marcheis be certaine youre leigijs of the surnames of Doddis, Charltonis and Mylburnis, undir the cure of Schir Rauf Fenwik, quhilkis on the 6 day of this instant Marche hes cumin within the grund of Teviotdale, reft and spoilzeit sindry gudis, murdryst fyve men, and utheris left in perrell of deid; albeit We, on oure side, have done sic diligence to caus gude will be kepit on the Bordowris for oure parte, that, as We belief, thaire is na just cause of complaynt aganis Ws. Praying Yow heirfore, derrest uncle, to cause reformatioun of thir attemptatis be haistelie providit, as accordis of resoun, baith for our honouris, and wele of oure Realmes and liegijs; considering that at the desire of youre last writing, send unto Ws with Rothissay herald, We have youre pleasure drawin away all occasioun of breke fra oure Bordouris for oure parte. Fother, derrest Uncle, We refer to oure Ambassaiatouris, quha will opin at lentht all thir materis unto Yow, to quham ye pleise gif credence, as to Oure self. Richt Excellent, Rucht Hie, and Mychty Prince,oure derrest Uncle and Bruthir, We pray God have Yow evir in His keping. Gevin at oure Palyse of Falkland, the 18 day of Marche.

Your lovyng Brother and Nepho, James Rex.[4]

After this exchange they got down to business once more. The border dispute brought out disagreement over lands previously adjudged to belong to Scotland and the English suggested that the French king be asked to arbitrate. The Scots however wanted the pope. "What pope?" asked the Duke of Norfolk, "the pope of Rome or the pope of Canterbury?" At which the bishop of Aberdeen reproved the duke. In the end Henry gave way to the Scots for the sake of the peace.

The bishop of Aberdeen wrote secretly to Thomas Cromwell, the First Secretary;

Schir. I praye you remembre the wowrdis betuix yow and me anentis my Masteris mariage, and be solistar and dresser yerof, as ye schew to me ye sould do. Now is the tym to solist,for our Imbassatoris ar in Fraunce for the samyn mater. Therfor I pray yow hartly to have the Kingis mynd therintill, for it is an article of my secreit credence, as the King Hymself knawis. His Grace ma perfetly wnderstand my Masteris gude and hartly mynd to Hym be mony wayis: therfor I dowt nocht bot His Grace will do now, as appertenis to an nobill Prince and kynd wncle till do for his part, in all thingis belangand my Masteris weill honor and proffeit.I pray yow keip secreit fra all persone the persuasioun of meting, bot fra the Kingis Grace allanerly; sa that nowlder wdyr man, Inglese nor Scotis, have wnderstanding therof, for diverse gude causis as I can schaw yow. Our writingis ar endit; therfor necessar is that we cum to the Kingis Grace, and have commoning with His Henese for our leif and departing. And Jhesus be your kepar.

your hartly and gud frend
Bischope of Abirden

Because I will mak na uther Secretar in thir materis bot my self, ye may excuse my ewill hand.[5]

The discussion with the council continued to be inconclusive and it was decided that one of the Scots should return to Edinburgh to acquaint

James with the situation and obtain further instructions. Robert Reid, abbot of Kinloss, was chosen for the mission.

Reid then returned to Scotland on the 5th or 6th May bearing Henry's reply to king James. The discussions were concluded after his departure. John Rokewood writing to Lord Lisle, the deputy of Calais, about the possible visit of Henry to France, remarked that "there have been many great days between them (the Scots) and the Council but nothing is yet concluded. There is an abbot of Scotland, who is riding to the king of Scots, and will return hither in post with an answer."

Bishop Stewart, meanwhile, getting somewhat impatient of the delay wrote again to Cromwell:

Gude Sir, I commend me hertlieto You. Ye will pleis be rememberit at oure last conventioune it was commonit that ye and I suld have spoken togidder on Friday at evin, or Satterday in the morning, and to have had fianall resolutioun of our materis as I belevit. I waittit therupoune, bot I knaw you sa gretely occupijt, that I may excuise. Prayande you, Sir, yat ye will commende my hertly prayeris to the Kingis Grace, and solist my gude and haisty despesche. I have necessair service of my Maisteris ado at hame, and wes directit here as ane man, mare of credence nor of wisdome; and in gude faith desiris, without fraude or dissimulatioun, to have hertlie and gude peax betuix baith the Princes, without ony dishonour or inconvenient to ony of thame, as I schew to the Kingis Grace at lenth, and als to his Counsaill: prayande you herfor to have the Kingis Grace mynde herintill, for my haisty depesche may be profitt to baith the Princes, as I beleif; and I pray you think never we will brek our peax with you. Tharfor (trepidaverunt ubi non erat timor) I write this in hamely and grose maner to you, as to my friend and bruther; havande traiste of your Maister, as I have of myne, quhilk is and salbe evir to halde thame in hertly kyndnes. And Jhesu be youre kepare.

Your gud Frend,
Bischope of Aberden.[6]

Soon after Reid's departure agreement was, in fact, reached and the treaty of London was signed on 11th May. The following day a separate treaty was made for the restoration of the castle of Edryngton called Cawmill and for the abode in England of the Douglases - the earl of Angus, his brother George and his uncle Archibald.

The bishop of Aberdeen, having secured safe conduct to return to London if it should prove necessary, left the city on 18th May with a party of fifty persons. On 30th June James ratified the treaty at Holyrood House in the presence of two thousand persons including three of Henry's councillors, the Prior of Duresme Monastery, Mr. Thomas Magnus and Mr. William Frankeleyn. On the 6th July Reid was commissioned to carry the ratification to Henry VIII. He returned to London soon after the 9th July to receive the oath of the English king to observe the treaty. The treaty was duly ratified by Henry VIII on the 2nd August 1534 at the Black Friars, Guildford "in the presence of Robert, abbot of Kinloss, ambassador of Scotland; Sir Thomas Audeley, Chancellor; Stephen, bishop of Winchester; Thomas, duke of Norfolk; Henry, earl of Northumberland; Henry, earl of Cumberland; Thomas Cromwell, the King's secretary; Sir William Fitzwilliam; Edward Fox, clerk, the King's almoner and Richard Simpson, dean of the Chapel". At the same time the abbot also delivered letters from James and from Queen Margaret, Henry's sister, to the king. Later he dined with the imperial ambassador to England.

On his return to Scotland Reid bore replies from Henry both to James and to his sister Margaret. To James the English king wrote thanking him for "your kynde and lovyng letters by the handes of your trustie Counsaillour and Ambassadour the Abbote of Keinlosse".[7] After acknowledging James' ratification of the treaty and confirming his own, Henry went on to express his expectation that together they would be able to prevail against any enemy and that their peoples would enjoy the peace which he would keep and trusted James would also. To his sister he wrote that "having receyved your lovyng and kynde letters addressed unto Us by the Reverende Father in God th'Abbote of Kenlosse" he perceives her love toward him and is sure of her wish to have perpetual peace between their realms, hinting that it is up to her to see that her son keeps to the terms agreed upon.[8]

At the treaty of Rouen in 1517 a future match for the young king had been considered between James and a French princess but no further action was taken at the time. Many years later, on the 6th April 1530, a commission was appointed by the Scots to negotiate a marriage with the king of France's eldest daughter, Madeleine. Many other possible brides had been suggested for the Scottish king, including Mary Tudor, but the latter was never a very real prospect. The negotiations for the marriage of King James to Madeleine, however, were broken off on account of the princess' ill health. The Scots now turned their thoughts to an alliance with the emperor. Up to that time such an alliance had been impossible owing to the treaties between Scotland and France. James had not altogether given up hope of obtaining the hand of the princess Madeleine in marriage but, while he was in London, Reid felt able to assure the imperial ambassador that there seemed little chance of such an outcome. He also discussed with the ambassador the position of Ireland. Reid appears to have been uncertain about the situation there but believed that his king had an understanding with the Irish and that he was not prepared to relinquish his claim to Ireland.

All now being concluded and with no more business to be undertaken in the English capital, Reid returned to Scotland laden with gifts of silver vessels as tokens of esteem. Embassies such as he had undertaken, and would undertake in future, undoubtedly added to his material wealth in respect of such gifts but the cost of the embassy itself fell largely to his own purse and must have been a considerable drain on his resources despite his being the holder of several ecclesiastical benefices and state appointments. Moreover he was, unlike some others in similar position, never miserly and was generous both to his relatives and others in need. The improvements he made to his monastery and later to his diocese must also have been a drain on his finances.

Robert Reid must have become quite saddle sore from the journeys between Edinburgh and London which would have taken weeks rather than days in each direction. He would not, of course, have travelled on his own. When kings moved from place to place the palace moved with them and a vast retinue of soldiers, servants and baggage would descend upon the household of some unfortunate baron who would be required to feed the invading host and to feel honoured in so doing. The abbot of Kinloss would have been accompanied by a more modest retinue but would, no doubt, have brought along his personal servant, his chaplain, who might have also acted as secretary, and his cook as well as whatever he might need in the way of comforts on the journey, and been provided with an escort of men-at-arms for his protection from robbers. The original party on leaving Scotland had been "well apparelit in all sorts, with 9 mules in thair caryage and hyngand at thame bellis of silver overgilt with gold, 30-50 persons and 70 horses". Normally the abbot would expect to receive hospitality from religious houses in the course of his journey. Although within Scotland and on journeys on the continent such expectations could have been realised, in England after 1530 it may not have been so easy. Even though Thomas Cromwell had not effected the dissolution of all the monasteries by this time, many would have disappeared either by force or voluntarily, requiring Reid and his retinue to seek hospitality wherever they might find it. The uneasy state of relations between the two countries might well have given English lords pause before admitting a Scot to their castle and a Scot pause before requesting such admission. This may have only applied to the lords temporal and it would have been unlikely that a cleric would have been denied hospitality in an age that still had a superstitious respect for men of the cloth, whatever their nationality. Moreover men on diplomatic missions would only have travelled after receiving letters of safe conduct from both their own sovereign and the one to whom the were accredited.

After his return from England Reid was again a lord commissioner of parliament on three occasions in the following two months of August and September 1534 and auditor of the accounts of the comptroller and of the lord high treasurer of Scotland in October. It was at about this time that he acquired the house of William Johnston who had fled abroad after being charged with heresy. He also obtained half the escheat of £26.1.3/4 of Jonet Wik, a bastard.

Reid and the bishop of Aberdeen had worked closely together during their mission to England. The abbot now acquainted the bishop with the work of Ferrerio at Kinloss and probably introduced the two men to one another. This resulted in an interchange of scholars between the monastery and the university of Aberdeen. Acquainted with both the bishop of Aberdeen and the abbot of Kinloss, Ferrerio expressed the view that "between hope and fear" the bishop and Robert Reid were the only two men who had been able to obtain a "peace surpassing all expectation from an angry nation" (England).

iii. Betrothal of James V

The abbot of Kinloss continued to be held in high regard both by his monarch and by the pope. He is said to have been on an embassy to Pope Paul III at this time and on a number of subsequent occasions but there are no contemporary records of such visits and it is unlikely that they were ever made. At home as papal commissary judge and executor he dispensed John Grant and Margaret Grant both of Moray diocese, who were related within the third and fourth degree of consanguinity, from any impediment to marriage. Also as papal mandatory he inducted Andrew Home, clerk of St. Andrews diocese, into possession of the teinds of the parish church of Lauder. In government he was again a lord commissioner of parliament in which he was elected a lord of the articles and was chosen by the lords spiritual for raising the taxation of £6000 granted to the king for his marriage. He was again royal commissioner for holding the exchequer.

It was the marriage of the king that was now to take up much of the abbot's time. Since the Emperor had now become reconciled to the English, Scotland was once more ready to resume the alliance with France. Henry, wishing to retain the favour of his nephew, had decided to confer on James the order of the Garter. James decided that the time had come for him, once again, to seek the bride who had first been chosen for him at the Treaty of Rouen in 1517 and whom he had again sought to acquire in 1530. He therefore entered into a correspondence with the French king in the hope that, with Henry and the Emperor now allied, Francis might overcome his reluctance and be ready to sacrifice his daughter on the altar of expediency. However, although Francis was anxious to oblige the Scots, he was still reluctant to part with his ailing daughter, Madeleine. As an alternative he offered the hand of Marie, the daughter of the Duke of Vendome, with a dowry of 100,000 livres and annual rents of 125,000 livres.

A diplomatic mission was then despatched to treat with the French king over the marriage. James Aikenheid was delegated to report his opinion of the bride-to-be "as if scho war his awin douhtyr" and to get confirmation of the tocher offered. The French king also agreed to send as many Frenchmen as James might require to be with the bride and also to return the castle of Dumbarton, which was in French hands, to the Scots.

However James, having received a portrait of Marie, decided that he would need further inducement to accept such a bride! The ships bearing the ambassadors, including the Bishop of Aberdeen and the duke of Albany, who were to make all the arrangements for the marriage, had already set sail. He decided, therefore, to send the abbot of Kinloss with further instructions and wrote to Francis "desiring credence" for the Abbot. Reid was to ask the French king for an additional pension of 20,000 livres, the order of St. Michael and the surrender of Dunbar, which was occupied by French troops. He also demanded that the privileges enjoyed by the Scots in Dieppe be extended to other French ports. The ambassadors were to obtain as great a tocher as they could from the king 'to compensate for delays and expenses of the last war with the English, when the French gave no assistance'. In return James offered the duchy of Ross, the lordships of Ardmannoch, Galloway and Strathearn and the earldoms of Orkney and Fife.

The ships bearing the bishop of Aberdeen having sailed, Reid proceeded overland through England either following or in company with the royal secretary, Sir Thomas Erskine. He was thus able to be present at the ceremony at Windsor when, on the 24th August 1535, Henry conferred the Order of the Garter on the Scottish king as a part of his efforts to detach him from the French alliance. Reid and Erskine then crossed to France to join the other ambassadors at the French court.

There would appear to have been some hard bargaining. The French king was reluctant to increase the 200,000 francs, already agreed, by the sum of 15,000 demanded, and there was haggling over the consent of the French parliament and Royal Chamber. Moreover when the ambassadors went to La Fere in Picardy to fetch the princess for her betrothal at Digoin she failed to go and 'difficulties' arose. The contract was not concluded. There was also talk of the princess being deformed and described as a 'humpback'. The Scottish deputation felt that they could not accept the French king's terms without further consulting their sovereign.

Once again Reid was the man chosen, together with secretary Erskine, to return to Scotland for James' answer. They took with them a message from the bishop of Aberdeen informing James of Henry VIII's "good will" toward the marriage. To this James replied that he "is glad to hear of Henry's good mind in furthering his marriage, and thanks him for his advice to Sir Thomas Erskine and Robert, abbot of Kinloss, bearers of these presents. Asks him to continue his assistance. Will not fail to keep semblable correspondence of entire favour and kindness in all things tending to the honour and weal of Henry and his subjects, to which he is bound by the natural bond of love and the late league of amity. Desires credence for Erskine and the abbot".[9]

Having considered their report James sent Reid and Erskine back to France to revoke Albany's commission and to give the ambassadors his resolution on doubtful matters. In his reply, James required the ambassadors, among other demands, to seek for a tocher as high as possible but to accept the 200,000 francs if they could obtain no better; to obtain as large a pension as possible; to require the surrender of Dunbar with munitions and artillery; to accept the conjunct fee if no better could be obtained; to solicit those persons that will come to Scotland to be of "sobir nummyr and chaste" and to confirm the extension of Scottish influence from Dieppe to other ports. His procurators were to be the

Duke of Albany, the earl of Moray, the bishop of Aberdeen and the abbot of Kinloss.

The two men once more stopped off in England on their way back to France, at the end of 1535, with a letter from James to Henry. This letter informed the English king that he had it in mind to revoke the commission to Albany to contract a marriage with Marie, the duke of Vendome's daughter, and pursue once more a union with Madeleine. They also took with them a letter from his sister, Queen Margaret, telling Henry how pleased she had been at the previous reception of the two ambassadors and asking him to receive them well again. Whilst at Windsor Robert Reid showed Henry the brief that the Pope had written to James expressing his (the pope's) desire to deprive the English king of his kingdom following the split with Rome. In the circumstances this was, perhaps, not an altogether diplomatic move. Reid also had a meeting with Cromwell who assured them that Henry and the Emperor now had a good understanding. Reid was unable to meet Lord Lisle, to whom he bore a letter, as he and Erskine were in a hurry to leave in order to reach the French king at Lyon.

Before leaving Reid obtained a licence to purchase twenty-four horses for King James.

Having greater trust in Reid and Erskine than the other ambassadors, James had authorised Reid to be his procurator for the marriage with Marie. It seems that he placed more faith in Reid and Erskine to safeguard his interests than he did the other two ambassadors. Albany was informed that James had learned the cause of the delay in the wedding arrangements from Reid and Erskine and had agreed that he would restore the dowry in the event of Marie's death, which was one of the points at issue. The treaty for the marriage of Marie de Bourbon, eldest daughter of the duke of Vendome, with James V, was finally made at Cremieu, 6 March. It was confirmed on 29 March 1535 between the Scottish ambassadors and for France, Francois, cardinal of Tournon; Antoine du Bourg, chancellor of France; Anne de Montmorency, grand master of France and Philip Chabot, count of Buzancou and admiral of France.

On Reid's return through England in April 1536 Secretary Cromwell paid him the sum of £23.6.8.

Meanwhile, the day after the execution of Anne Boleyn, Francis offered his daughter Madeleine in marriage to Henry who, fortunately for the young princess, decided that he would not marry outside England (a decision he clearly forgot later when contracting to Anne of Cleves) and in any case Madeleine was too young.

For a time, before finally committing himself to Marie of Vendome, James had been hoping to marry Margaret Erskine, the wife of Sir Robert Douglas of Lochleven by whom he already had a bastard son, but the pope Paul III who, as cardinal Alessandro Farenese, had been something of a libertine himself before his elevation to the papacy, was now a reformed character and refused to grant Margaret a divorce.

All was now ready for the Scottish king to cross to France to claim his bride. The abbot of Kinloss was to accompany the royal party.[10]

The royal party took ship at Pittenweem on 23rd July 1536 but they were forced to return by the weather. They eventually departed from Kirkcaldy on the first of September 1536, landing at Dieppe on the tenth. James then proceeded to Vendome in disguise and did not like what he saw of the lady he was contracted to wed. He was expected at Lyon on the fifth of October where, despite his unconventional behaviour, Francis ordered that he be received as a king should be. Meeting the French king between Tours and St. Saphorin James asked, once again for the hand of his daughter, Madeleine.

Despite Francis' misgivings regarding Madeleine's state of health he eventually gave way and agreed to the wedding of his daughter to the Scots King.

The marriage of the King of Scotland to the daughter of the King of France was duly solemnised in the church of Notre Dame on the first of January 1537 with all the pageantry that such occasions demanded. What part the abbot of Kinloss played is not recorded since there were so many more important people involved to claim the attention of the annalists.

The happy couple left France at the end of April and landed at Leith on 26th May making a triumphal progress to Holyrood Palace.

The fears of the French king proved only too well founded and Madeleine died on 7th July 1537 within a couple of months of returning to Scotland.

Cardinal Beaton was then sent to negotiate another French marriage for James and he agreed with the French king on the selection of Marie, daughter of Claude of Guise-Lorraine, whose first husband had died only a short while before the death of Madeleine. This was a further blow to the ambitions of the English king who had been hoping to make the lady his own bride and it must have galled him to be displaced by his nephew.

The marriage took place the following May 1538 by proxy. Marie arriving to join her husband at St. Andrew's in June. She was to bear him two sons and a daughter. Only the latter survived the father, a fact that was to have a profound effect on the future of Scottish politics and perhaps even its church. It was also to engage the future services of Robert, bishop of Orkney.

Notes

1. Calendar of State Papers of Henry VIII. (1863) Part iv. CCLIV p.664
2. Ibid. CCLV p.665
3. Robert Lindsay of Pitscottie: "Cronicles of Scotland" (1814). p.351
4. Calendar of State Papers of Henry VIII CCLVI p.665
5. Ibid. CCLIX p.668
6. Ibid. CCLX p.669
7. Ibid. CCLXIV p.673
8. Ibid. CCLXV p.674
9. State Papers of Henry VIII vol. ix 1043 p.361
10. On the 12th September Reid's name appears among the list of auditors of the accounts of the lord high treasurer of Scotland but clearly he could not have been present in person and his name was presumably added because he would normally have been a member of the auditory commission. His name also appears as a witness at Perth on the twentieth of November but it is exceedingly unlikely that he would have returned to Scotland by then especially as he was absent from the College of Justice for fifteen months at this time.

4 Sext

Quam diecta tabernacula tu: concupiscit, et deficit anima me in atria Domini.

i. Bishop of Orkney

In the spring of 1541 Bishop Robert Maxwell of Orkney died only months after the king, accompanied by a number of noblemen and Cardinal Beaton, had visited the islands. (According to legend that was not the first time that King James V had visited Orkney. There is a tale told that he had previously arrived in the islands in disguise and lodged with a family in Sandwick. The family only discovered the king's identity when he was seen combing his hair with a golden comb. Before leaving them he knighted the head of the family who thereafter claimed the title of 'earl'!)

On the 5th April 1541 the king wrote to the pope proposing that, the bishop of Orkney having departed this life, Robert Reid, Abbot of Kinloss, should succeed him. He explained to the pope - in case the pontiff was ignorant of the geography of the region - that the Isles of Orkney were not far below the pole and situated near Norway, Denmark and Germany. He explained that the catholic faith and laws were little observed there, which may well have been true. Robert, of the Cistercian abbey of Kinloss, he told the pope, was altogether the best man to correct the situation. He added that he would wish the new bishop to provide a pension of 800 marks to John Stewart, one of the king's own illegitimate sons, and also requested that the bishop should be permitted to discard the habit of a monk and assume the garb of a bishop as more fitting for his position both in company with the king and among the Orkney islanders.

For the time being Reid would remain as Commendator of both Kinloss and Beauly. As a bishop he could no longer be styled abbot but retained all the administrative powers in respect of the monastery and priory. It was not until 1550 that he resigned the commendatorship of Kinloss in favour of his nephew Walter Reid. Even this was a mere formality, since Walter was still under age, but it ensured the eventual succession to one of his own kin whom he believed would continue the good work that he, and abbot Crystal before him, had begun. Beauly, of which he was already commendator, he never resigned. It was only after Robert's death that Walter was provided to Beauly following an act of parliament that allowed the provision to the nearest of kin of a prelate with that prelate's benefice.

Before leaving Kinloss, in 1541 the abbot returned to Alexander Bannerman of Watertoun the duties on Watertoun which Walter, Lord of St. John, had made over to the abbot of Kinloss, together with those of Ellon, Craighead and others, which St. John had inherited from Robert Meldrum of Fyvie. Later in 1544, with his nephew Walter, he constituted John Grant of Freuchie principal bailie of Kinloss. In 1552, he and Walter sued John Murray, Robert Tulloch, Syme Merchell and Patrick Anderson for repayment of fishing of the Findhorn.

Ferrerio, who had returned to Kinloss in 1541, remained there until 1544 when he left Scotland for the last time.

Pope Paul III replied to the king's request by, providing "Robert, abbot of the monastery of the Blessed Virgin Mary of Kinloss, in the order of priesthood and counsellor of king James, to the bishopric of Orkney vacant by the death of Bishop Robert (Maxwell), but not ceasing to rule over the monastery", by sending letters to the king, the chapter, clergy, peoples, all vassals of the diocese and the archbishop of St. Andrew's (Cardinal Beaton). In order that Robert Reid might live in a state commensurate with his pontifical rank he permitted the new bishop to discard the habit of a monk and assume the dress of a bishop, as requested by the king. He was also able to retain all those sources of income which had been so helpful to him in the past, the priory of Beauly and the rights of regress of the vicarage of Kirkcaldy and the fruits of the canonry and prebendary as sub-dean of Moray. The pension of £20 awarded to James Thornton cleric of St. Andrew's, who had been procurator for Baudevan when he exchanged the priory of Beauly with Reid, was cancelled and a new one of £20 from the fruits of the bishopric substituted. It was agreed that John Stewart should receive 800 merks from the fruits of the bishopric. The new bishop was also formally absolved from "any whatever excommunication". The pope also wrote to "his dear son, Robert, Elect of Orkney" on 16th October 1541. (Appendix 1)

Reid's consecration took place in the church of Grey Friars in Edinburgh, the same church in which he had been admitted to the Cistercian order, on the first Sunday in Advent, 27th December 1541.

Which bishop or bishops performed the ceremony is not recorded but Cardinal Beaton, his own metropolitan, was away in France and Reid would have been unlikely to have requested Gavin Dunbar, archbishop of Glasgow who was no friend of Beaton's. There remained six other possibles, Stewart of Aberdeen, Hepburn of Brechin, Chisholm of Dunblane, Crichton of Dunkeld, Hepburn of Moray (his bishop as abbot of Kinloss but not a man that Reid would have found congenial) and Cairncross of Ross. The bishop of Aberdeen would seem the most likely one to have been chosen.

During 1541, before his consecration, Reid is said to have paid his first visit to Orkney and immediately begun to plan the restoration of old buildings and the erection of new ones commensurate with the dignity of the diocese and his office as its bishop. The state of the church in Orkney at this time, as well as the condition of the people throughout the islands, was one that required the energies of an able pastor and administrator to repair, as the king's letter to the pope had made clear. It was with this in mind that had caused James to choose Robert Reid to succeed Maxwell. The legacy of the battle of Summerdale and the chaos caused by the feuding Sinclairs was still having its affect on the islanders and it is probable that the king had observed for himself the need for a strong hand when he visited the islands. There is a suggestion that Ferrerio accompanied the bishop elect but it is unlikely that he had returned from Paris in time to do so.

ii. The bishop as architect

Now, at last, at the beginning of August 1544, two years after his consecration as bishop, Robert Reid was sufficiently free from affairs of state to make his second visit to his diocese. It may seem strange that such a long interval elapsed between the time of his consecration and Reid's first visit as bishop to his diocese. As will be seen later, his time had been fully occupied with judicial matters and affairs of state. It may be that during the early months of 1543, when he had retired to his abbey of Kinloss, that he paid an unrecorded visit to his diocese.

At Kinloss and Beauly he would have had experience of both the lowlands and the highlands, now for the first time, for any period, he was to become acquainted with island life. He would have found that, although inroads were beginning to be made into the old norse system of land tenure, much still remained of the udal laws which had governed the islands for centuries. As a lawyer he must have found this interesting and perhaps challenging, especially as so many of the cases he had had to hear in the south dealt with the hereditary rights and the ownership of property.

Most towns of the period were dominated by a church and perhaps a castle or manor house, and possibly a few of the richer merchants houses, the only buildings of stone. Around them would cluster the houses of of the poor, made largely of wood and plaster. Kirkwall would have been no exception although in Orkney, devoid of wood for building, the houses of the poor too would have been of stone, but small and crowded together in narrow lanes. When the king had visited Orkney in the episcopacy of bishop Maxwell, tradition has it that he was accommodated in a house in what is now Victoria Street, owned by the bishop and possibly also occupied by Maxwell. The Bishop's palace may well have been in too bad a state of repair for occupancy. Nevertheless, even in a state of disrepair it would have been one of the more prominent features of the town.

Bishop Reid began to put into practice the ideas for rebuilding that he had formed on his earlier visit.

Hossack[1] disputes the tradition, however, and quotes several authorities to suggest that the old palace was still in a sufficiently good state of repair to accomodate not only the king but his large retinue during their visit.

There is no contemporary evidence for Reid's role in the various building enterprises with which he has been credited by later writers but there are, nevertheless, indications of his hand in the work, especially when it is remembered how he had improved the buildings at Kinloss and Beauly.

The Bishop's Palace, that would have been in existence from shortly after the time that the cathedral was built in 1137, was, in all probability, in a poor state of repair when Reid arrived in Kirkwall.

The original palace was a simple rectangular hall with an undercroft and it was in this hall that the Norwegian king, Haakon, died after the battle of Largs in 1263. It may also have been that the Maid of Norway died in the palace on her way to marry the Prince of Wales in 1290.

When Bishop Reid arrived he set about the restoration of the building. He added to it an imposing round tower at the north west corner and buttressed the western wall of the building which appears to have been sagging. The tower contained the bishop's own apartments and was strongly fortified, with embrasures for firearms defence. This latter was probably a precaution against any further trouble from the Sinclairs, Lord William Sinclair having seized the palace in 1526 and been ordered to return it to the bishop by the Privy Council. It will be recalled that the building he had had erected at Kinloss for his accommodation was also a round tower, evidently a form of domestic architecture for which he had formed a preference.

The presence of Reid's coat of arms and initials on various parts of the building, noted in later centuries, has been given as evidence of his responsibility for the work. The round tower is especially ascribed to Reid on account of his coat of arms (a stag's head covered by a mitre) and his initials R.R. on the square chamber at the top of the tower and also on the supposition that the statue in a niche on this tower is of the bishop himself. This latter is now no longer regarded as representing Robert Reid, the statue being certainly much older than the tower. Dr. Barbara Crawford [2] has put forward a well-argued case for its being a likeness of Earl Rognvald, the builder of St. Magnus Cathedral, which Reid had had removed from the cathedral and placed on the tower. Why he should have done so is not known. It may be that, having seen, on his many visits to England, the desecration that such monuments had undergone since the suppression of the monasteries by Henry VIII, he had decided that St. Rognvald would be a lot safer high up on his tower should any similar catastrophe occur in Orkney! The smaller of the square towers is also said to have carried Reid's coat of arms and initials at one time.

Whilst the palace was being restored and the tower built, Reid may have occupied the house in Victoria Street that Maxwell is said to have used as a palace. This house too bore the initials and arms of Robert Reid as well as those of bishop Maxwell. It may be however that the stones bearing these initials were built into this house at a later date and that bishop Maxwell had in fact occupied the old palace. Another house south of this 'bishop's palace' in Victoria Street also once bore the initials and arms of Robert Reid as well as those of Murray (R.R. and J.M.) over the doorway and this may perhaps have been built by Reid on his arrival, before work on the restoration of the palace was completed.

The restoration of St. Olaf's Church in what is now Bridge Street Wynd is also credited to Reid as his name and arms were, at one time, found on the walls. The original St. Olaf's was believed to have been erected on the bay by Earl Rognvald Brusison, in memory of his foster-father King Olaf, and to have given its name to Kirkwall (Kirkiu-vagr, the Creek of the Church).

Although the presence of Reid's arms and initials are not in any way conclusive evidence that he was responsible for any of these buildings - since his arms also appeared on the bishop's palace at Elgin where he had been a canon - tradition is strongly in his favour. His reputation as a builder at Kinloss and Beauly would tend to support the claims. All that now remains of old St. Olaf's church is the doorway to be seen in Bridge Street Wynd and part of a window which was removed and placed in the present St. Olaf's in Dundas Crescent as an aumbrey and in which the reserved sacrament is still held. After Reid's day St. Olaf's was, in time, no longer in use as a church and became in turn a tenement, a carpenter's shop and a warehouse.

A building behind Broad Street was erected about this time - "a Court of Houses to be a College for the Instructing the Youth of this Country in Grammar and Philosophy", according to Wallace in 1688 [3]. There is no contemporary evidence to support this statement made 150 years after the building was started. Reid's interest in the education of the young, however, makes the suggestion that he was responsible for the building highly probable. A building on the site of what is now Tankerness House in Broad Street may also have been erected in Reid's time as some of the walls of the present house show evidence of older construction. The present building, originally two dwellings, having been completed during the time of Reid's successor, bishop Bothwell.

Finally it is believed that Reid added three bays to the west end of the cathedral together with a magnificent porch and doorway. There is considerable doubt as to the extent of Reid's involvement in the extension of the cathedral. Fawcett [4] however considers that it is more likely that the work was undertaken in the time of Bishop Andrew (1477-1508) and may have been started even earlier by his predecessor, Bishop Tulloch. It has been claimed that the coat of arms over the main west door is that of Bishop Andrew but its present state does no more than suggest the presence of a mitre with nothing else distinguishable, so that it might have born the arms of any bishop. The original west porch was moved to take account of the lengthened nave. The one addition to the church that most authorities agree to be the work of Bishop Reid is the doorway on the south aisle at the start of the extension to the nave. Above this is a shield that probably bore Reid's coat of arms. Whether or not Reid was responsible for the extension of the cathedral the presence of this doorway suggests that he may have had a hand in its completion.

It is possible that Reid brought the artist, Andrew Bairham, to Orkney to decorate the cathedral with frescoes as he had done at Kinloss. Alas, if it were so, no trace of them remain today. Reid is also believed to have had his gardener, Guillaume Lubias, improve the palace gardens and generally to introduce horticulture to Orkney.

iii. Reform of the chapter

Having dealt with the diocesan buildings, the new bishop turned his attention to those whose duties were to be carried out within them. He found that the cathedral chapter was in urgent need of reconstitution. The chapter he inherited consisted of only six canons and as many chaplains none of whose duties were set down in writing or, if they had been in the past, no record of such a document was to be found. A cathedral church such as St. Magnus was, in those days, expected to maintain a staff of clergy to serve the offices and, in addition, to provide pastoral care to the people of the diocese. A criticism levelled at bishop Reid, in the light of contemporary practice, is his insistence on enlarging the cathedral staff whilst seeming to ignore the needs of the parishes. This is not altogether fair since in the medieval catholic church a bishop was, or was intended to be, the shepherd of his flock. It was his personal responsibility to see that their pastoral needs were catered for. The parish priest acted only under the jurisdiction and direction of his bishop and had none of the independence of action expected of the protestant ministry of our day. The provision of Reid was to the church of Orkney not, in fact, to the diocese which was considered simply as the territory belonging to the church. The distinction is, perhaps, a fine one but one that nevertheless emphasises Reid's role as pastor to the whole of the church in Orkney and its people.

However, apart from being a bishop, Reid had become a national statesman with duties extending far beyond the bounds of the diocese, clearly therefore he was often in no position to take personal care of his flock at all times. It was therefore all the more important that he should see that a properly constituted body of clergy was in place to act in his absence. It is easy today to see the failings of such a system and it might be reasonable to condemn Reid for accepting an office to which he could give only a fraction of his time. It has to be remembered that the king chose Robert Reid for the job, not only because he believed him to be the man to restore the standing of the catholic church in that diocese, but also so that he might have the status to act as his representative among the councils of Europe.

On the 28th October 1544 a formal constitution was produced for the establishing of a new chapter and for the conduct of the offices in the cathedral church of 'St. Magnus.

The "FOUNDATION and ERECTION of certain OFFICES in the CATHEDRAL CHURCH of ORKNEY, for the Service of God, by ROBERT, Bishop of ORKNEY".[5]

This provided for the appointment of a provost, six other dignitaries, seven other prebendaries, thirteen chaplains and six boys.

There followed a list of the stringent qualifications required of members of the chapter, the duties associated with each office and the names of those appointed who fulfilled the bishop's requirements:

The Provost shall be a Doctor or, at least a Bachelor, of Divinity and to be the first after the bishop - "inquisitor heredice pravitatis" (responsible for seeking out and indicting heretics). Therefore he is to be the man principally responsible for the diocese in the bishop's frequent absences. He is to correct canons and to preach in the cathedral in the vernacular at least four times a year. He would be the prebend of the Holy Trinity with the vicarage of South Ronaldsay and have the subsistence from the church of Burwick appropriated to him. The man appointed was Malcolm Halcro (or Hawcrow), a former fellow student of the bishop's at St. Andrew's who was not, in fact, a Doctor of Divinity but a biblical scholar, a Bachelor of Sacred Letters. He was also the archdeacon of Shetland. The fourth chaplain was his stallery.

[Members of the chapter were allotted 'stallaries' from among the chaplains. These were priests who would occupy the stall in the chancel of the dignitary to whom they were allotted, in the absence of that dignitary.][6]

The Archdeacon shall be, at least, a Master of Arts who will also be required to discharge the duties of the bishop over the clergy and people in the latter's absence. He too is to preach in the vernacular at least four times a year - or be fined. The vicarage of Birsay and the chaplainry of St. Olaf within the cathedral with the subsistence from the church of Harray to be appropriated to him. John Tyrie was appointed Archdeacon, that is to say Archdeacon of Orkney; (Malcolm Hacrow, the provost was, in addition, Archdeacon of Shetland). The fifth chaplain to be his stallary.

The Precentor, responsible for the music, to be a Master of Arts or graduate in some other faculty and well versed in chant. He is to conduct the choir, to regulate the celebration of masses and the employment of singers in chapter for the following week, and engage choirboys. The prebend of Orphir and the vicarage of Stenness is appropriated to him.

His stallary is that of the fifth chaplain. Sir Nicholas Halcro was appointed precentor.

The Chancellor should be a Doctor of Laws or at least a Bachelor of Canon Law from a flourishing university, fit to discharge justice in spiritual courts on the bishop's order. He is to lecture the canons in the chapter on canon law at least once a week on pain of being treated as non-resident and fined. He is to oversee the books of the choir and the register, to keep one key of the box containing the common seal and the key as well as the catalogue of the library and to attend the bishop, provost or canons whenever they wished to enter the library for study. The prebend of Lady in Sanday and the vicarage of Sanday to be appropriated to him. His stallary was that of the seventh chaplain. The Chancellor was Alexander Scott who had been a canon of the cathedral since 1539 and Rector of Westray since 1527.

The Treasurer to be a Master of Arts. He is to receive the treasury, ornaments, vestments, and precious objects on the receipt of the provost and at least four brethren at the time of his installation. He is to take care of the bread, wine, wax, oil and feed for the lights, to wash the linen of the high altar and the alters of Our Lady and the Holy Blood four times a year and the albs twice or thrice a year and to repair torn vestments. He is to keep the other key of the common seal. The rectory of St. Nicholas of Stronsay and the vicarage of Stronsay to be appropriated to him. The eighth chaplain to be his stallary. Sir Stephen Culross was appointed treasurer.

The Sub-dean to be a Master of Arts, well versed in both testaments. He should be fit to discharge the duties of Provost in the latter's absence in respect of correcting failures in the chapter. He is to preach three times a years and to be penitentiary for cases reserved for the bishop. The rectory of Hoy and the vicarage of Walls is appropriated to him and the ninth chaplain to be his stallary. Peter Houston, rector of Hoy since 1540, was appointed sub-dean.

The Subchanter (succentor) to be a priest well trained in chants and an organist. He is to deputise for the Precentor in the latter's absence and play the organ at vespers, high mass and during the Te Deum and Benedictus on all Sundays and feast days. The prebend of St. Colm (in Sanday) is appropriated to him. Magnus Strang was appointed subchanter. He had held the prebend of the Cross since 1531.

All seven prebendaries are to be canons, they are to sing both vespers and high mass on Sundays and double feasts, in turn, as ordered by the precentor, on pain of being fined. If the provost or any other four dignitaries celebrate the mass, two prebendaries shall be deacon and sub-deacon or assistants at vespers. They are obliged to be present at the chancellor's lectures or suffer the loss of their appointments. They are to have the following duties:

The prebendary of the Holy Cross to be the sacrist major, to watch over the horologe (the clock) and be responsible for the bell-ringing, to account to the bishop for the expense of incense and the lighting of the church and to see that the floor is kept clean. He had also to keep account of the glebes. The rectory of Cross kirk in Sanday is to be appropriated to him. The tenth chaplain is his stallary.

The prebendary of St. Magnus to be the confessor to the bishop's household as well as the provost, canons, prebendaries, chaplains and their servants at Eastertide, to minister the Body of Christ and to appoint and maintain the second choir-boy. The prebend of St. Magnus to be appropriated to him. Hugh Halcro, vicar of Walls from 1523 and parson of Ronaldsay from 1531 was appointed Prebendary of Holy Coss in 1544 but died in 1546.

The prebendary of St. John is to appoint and maintain the third choir-boy. The chaplainry of St. John within the cathedral is to be appropriated to him. Mr. Henry Bartoun was appointed to the prebendary of St. John in 1544. He was succeeded by Mr. James Annand in 1558 who resigned in 1560.

The prebendary of St. Mary to be master of works of the church, to attend to the roof and windows of the church. The chaplainry of St. Mary and the vicarage of Evie to be appropriated to him. The eleventh chaplain is his stallary. Mr. Walter Thomson was appointed in 1544.

The prebendary of St. Lawrence is to appoint and maintain the fourth choir-boy. The chaplainry of St. Lawrence to be appropriated to him. John Maxwell, chaplain of St. Catherine since 1541, was appointed and succeeded by Francis Bothwell in 1556.

The prebendary of St. Catherine is to appoint and maintain the fifth choir-boy. The prebend of the same name is allotted to him. David Cristisoun was prebendary of St. Catherine in 1544 and succeeded by Sir John Ryd in 1550.

The prebendary of St. Duthac which had been held by Sir David Fallowsdale from 1539 was awarded to Mr. Robert Malcolmson in 1544. He is to appoint and maintain the sixth choir-boy. The prebend of St. Duthac is allotted to him. (Both St. Lawrence and St. Duthac were in the parish of Sandwick).

The appointment of all the dignitaries, canonries and prebends are to be in the gift of the bishop.

The parish churches and teinds and all profits belonging to the rectories of St. Colm of Walls and of the Crosskirk in Westray and the vicarages of the parish churches of Sandwick and Stromness were to be assigned for everyday apportionment of the fourteen dignitaries and prebendaries. Thus no vicars were appointed to care for these parishes or those of Deerness and Rousay in 1544 and many other of the parishes only acquired vicars at a later date.

The following emoluments were allotted: to the provost and canons twelve pence for residence and attendance at four major canonical hours on principal double feasts commencing with the first vespers; eight pence for three major hours on Sundays and other double feasts and six pence for one major hour (matins) on remaining on ferial (non-festival) days throughout the year. These payments would be distributed by a canon and a prebendary elected, for a year for that purpose, by the chapter. The same two would collect the fruits and count the number of residents present every Saturday for the past week, which would then be entered by the notary. The provost and canons to begin their residence on the feast of All Saints and to be paid quarterly on 2nd February, 3rd May, 1st August and 1st November.

All the major dignitaries and the canons were obliged to reside for the greater part of the year and may not be absent for half the year; the subdean, subchantor and the prebendaries of Holy Cross and St. Mary should not be absent for one quarter of the year and the other prebendaries must be present for at least one quarter of the year. This was to ensure the presence of sufficient clergy to conduct the offices and preach. The non-residents may be absent only with the consent of the bishop and chapter and should pay a quarter of the fruits to the resident canons; the official and the bishop's vicar to keep the distributors informed of the payment in writing.

The canonry of St. Olaf would belong to the bishop who with the canons would take oath to observe the statutes of the foundation of the chapter. The third chaplain to be the bishop's stallary.

The chaplain of St. Peter to be the senior chaplain and the thirteen chaplains were to celebrate mass at dawn and the mass of St. Mary everyday and the mass of the Holy Blood on Thursdays and for the dead on every Monday throughout the year, taking it in turns.

The chaplain of St. Peter should be a Master of Arts, expert in grammar and examined by the provost, archdeacon, chancellor and sub-dean before being admitted. He would be the master of the grammar school and should take part in at least one, and preferably two, canonical hours in the choir wearing a surplice on solemn and feast days.

The chaplain of St. Augustine should be skilled in both chants and be examined in the same way as the subchantor. He was to be master of the sang school.

These two masters were to train all the choir-boys and also any poor who wish to be present serving at the altar without payment.

The nine chaplains who were to be stallaries of the bishop, dignitaries and prebendaries should be priests and will be presented to the bishop or bishop's vicar in things spiritual by their respective canons or prebendaries within two months of a vacancy. The provost, precentor and subchantor would examine them to ensure they were well trained in chant and reading. They should receive one chalder of victual a year and ten marks money as stipend, distributed daily, from the fruits of the vicarage of the cathedral church and from the endowment by Bishop Thomas and twelve pounds from the endowment by Kings James III and IV to be paid by the bishop for celebration of masses. The remaining two chaplains are those of St. Catherine and Holy Cross.

Those holding the positions of provost, dignitaries, canons, prebends, chaplains and vicarages of the choir were not to hold other positions at the same time and the chaplains of St. Peter and of St. Augustine who were to be in charge of the grammar and sang schools respectively may not hold any other benefice. Anyone holding more than one such position for two months, both benefices should be declared vacant.

There should be one sacrist to ring bells, light candles and bring water and fire. He should precede the procession wearing a surplice and bearing a white rod like a beadle. He would receive the customary income and forty shillings from the bishop.

The choirboys were to be torch bearers and to sing the responses, versicles etc. and would be examined by the precentor and subchantor but were to be appointed and maintained by the prebendaries as already described. They would be paid twenty shillings a year each.

All members of the chapter including the prebendaries would be allotted ground around the cathedral on which to build manses in which to live, within three years. In this way the bishop encouraged his chapter to reside around the precincts of the cathedral and establish a cathedral close in conformity with the structure of other diocesan communities.

In the parishes the bishop would appoint vicars pensionary to service the cure of souls whenever a vacancy arises and they would be paid ten marks and half a chalder of victuals a year with a manse from the fruits of the present act of foundation.

If the bishop were to infringe any of these statutes the provost and canons may appeal to a judge to procure redress. The statute of the chapter to be read by the subdean four times a year. It was approved by the bishop on the 28th October 1544 and signed by him, Nicholas Hacrow, Rector of Orphir; Stephen Culros, Rector of Stronsay; Peter Houston, Rector of Hoy; James Maxwell, Rector of St. Mary's Sanday; Malcolm Hawcrow as Archdeacon of Shetland and prebendary of the Holy Trinity and Magnus Strang, prebendary of St. Columba.

The Foundation Charter of the chapter was then sent by the bishop to his metropolitan, the archbishop of St. Andrew's, Cardinal Beaton who, as papal legate, confirmed it on 30th June 1545. It had previously been confirmed by the queen in council on the 30th April 1545.

Now having enlarged the chapter from one of the smallest in Scotland, barely the size of that for a collegiate church, to one that was comparable to that of any in the land, Reid was free to respond to the many other calls on his time. He could leave the care of his diocese in the hands of a body of clergy well qualified for the tasks allotted to them. As to the individual parishes, in appointing vicars pensionary, in addition to the rectors on the chapter who had supervisory responsibility for them and from which they drew their income, he had not, as some have suggested, ignored their requirements entirely. He did however appropriate the rectory of Ronaldsay and the vicarages of Sanday and Walls and three common churches to swell the cathedral coffers. It is true that his diocese was one of the smallest and one that lacked the revenues of the wealthier sees such as St. Andrew's, Glasgow or Aberdeen but the bishopric still held the bishop's lands throughout the islands from which it drew both rents and scat. However the size of the new chapter with its increased responsibilities and the extensive building works the bishop put in train must have been quite a drain on this limited income. Moreover, although Reid may have enjoyed a considerable personal income, from his various benefices and appointments, he was always ready to help those in need and personally employed the gardener and artist who would have added to the glory of his abbey and cathedral.

It is perhaps somewhat ironic that he should have been so strict in forbidding the holding of more than one benefice by his subordinate clergy when he himself held a number of far more responsible positions. He had however made sure that every aspect of the service and conduct of the cathedral and diocese was fully covered. In this way he ensured that an example of catholic practice was set for the citizens of the isles, to encourage them to practice their faith in full conformity with the teachings of catholic doctrine. How far he succeeded must be judged by the behaviour of the people of Orkney when confronted by the Reformation. There was, however, to be too little time for Robert Reid's reforms to have any lasting effect. It has been argued that this was, perhaps, just as well since his reforms have been criticised as concentrating on the reform of the cathedral chapter at the expense of the parishes. However, as has been shown, with the few exceptions reported, the bishop ensured the appointment of vicars for the every day cure of souls in the parishes. It would have been the overall responsibility of the chapter clergy, who benefitted from the fruits of those parishes, to see that they received pastoral care.

Mooney[7] has argued that Reid behaved in a high handed fashion in appropriating the emoluments of the prebend of St. John to the service of the cathedral staff. These he maintains had been specifically allotted to the maintenance of the fabric of the building which had, by royal charter, been invested in the Kirkwall Burgh Council. His contention rests on the belief that the cathedral was the property of the Earls of Orkney before the impigoration and that after King James III had acquired the earldom property he could legally dispose of it as he chose. Whether or not that original charter was legal, by now, time and repeated challenges must surely validate its present day status. If the charter assigning the church to the townsfolk of Kirkwall was valid then Bishop Reid had no power to assign the prebend of St. John except with the consent of the Burgh Council, which was responsible for applying the income therefrom to the upkeep of the fabric of the cathedral. However Reid makes little mention of the St. John prebend except to allot it to Mr. Henry Bartoun whilst requiring the Prebendary of St. Mary to be master of works and responsible for the fabric. It seems that not only did the crown accept the bishop's arrangements but that no objection was raised by the Burgh Council. The councillors were no doubt only too glad to have the responsibility for the day to day running of the cathedral taken off their hands, especially if the bishop, once notified of any defects, undertook to have the repairs done at his own expense. It would appear therefore that the prebend of St. John was being relieved of the expense of these repairs, at least during Reid's episcopate. Although the cathedral has remained the property of the Kirkwall Town Council (now invested in the Orkney Island Council), whatever Christian denomination has had use of the building has never been questioned as to their right to appoint ministers and arrange services according to their beliefs and traditions. It is doubtful if Reid's management of affairs could, or should, have been challenged as illegal at the time.

iv. The bishop and the Scottish Renaissance

It will be seen from the qualifications required for some of these appointments and the reforming of the 'sang school' that Reid attached great importance to the value of music in the offices of the church. Although few manuscripts of Scottish church music have come down to us there is evidence that the tradition of polyphonic church music was flourishing in pre-reformation church services in the great abbeys and cathedrals, many of which had choirs and sang schools. The works of those sixteenth century composers, such as Robert Carver and Robert Johnson, that have survived, are the equal of any of the period. St. Magnus Cathedral would then have resounded with their masses and anthems, precursors of the music to be heard there five hundred years later in the St. Magnus Festival of our day. It is in character with Robert, bishop of Orkney, that he should wish to have the offices sung in his cathedral to be of the finest, to the greater glory of God.

St. Magnus Cathedral today is the jewel in Orkney's crown. Small by comparison with most of the great cathedrals of the past but no less lacking in grandeur and excelling many in beauty, built as it was of the pale red sandstone found in the isles. Its romanesque pillars give to it an air of solidarity complemented by the graceful arches of the crossing which soar up toward the tower. It is at the same time both an impressive and an intimate building.

Imagine what it would have been like to have been present at a solemn Mass in the presence of the bishop in the middle of the sixteenth century. The church would have been free of the accumulated accretions of the past four centuries, the memorial plaques which break up the pure architecture of the aisles; the chairs that serve to shorten the height of the great pillars of the nave; the Victorian gothic pulpit and screen that diminish the space and grace of the choir; the microphones and loudspeakers that too often distort rather than enhance the human voice and, above all, the harsh electric lighting that destroys much of the mysterious beauty that the builders brought to their creation.

The building would have been lit by the light of candles that throw soft shadows across the aisles and cause the arches to sore to heaven; the embroidered vestments of the clergy, copes, chasubles and dalmatics, would glow with colour as the procession proceeded up the nave to the sanctuary, led by the cross bearer, flanked by candlebearing acolytes and followed by the choir intoning the psalms or filling the ancient building with the harmonies of a sacred anthem. Such a performance may have horrified the reformers as a piece of idolatrous theatricality but, to the layman in the congregation, experiencing those sights and sounds in the setting of the glorious architecture of St. Magnus cathedral, it must have brought a sense of awe and reverence.

Outwith his church, bishop Reid would, at the same time, have been encouraging the practice of the very best in all forms of cultural activity within his diocese. It is a legacy which Orkney has not neglected.

Robert Reid was an inheritor of the Scottish Renaissance. The three greatest poets of that time, Robert Henryson, William Dunbar and Gavin Douglas had flourished at the end of the fifteenth and start of the sixteenth centuries. Sir David Lyndsay, the poet and author of 'Ane Pleasant Satyre of the Thrie Estaitis', was very much Reid's contemporary. He had been "usher" to the young James V, and became Lyon King at Arms and a diplomat. He and Robert Reid would therefore have become acquainted at court. The bishop may not have had the works of these poets in his library but there is no reason to suppose that he would be unacquainted with them nor that he would have found anything in them that was unacceptable. One of them (Gavin Douglas) was, after all, also a bishop.

Although Reid had had a new building erected for the "College to teach Grammar and Philosophy" and had appointed masters from among the chaplains to the Grammar and Sang Schools, neither of these were new foundations. The founding of a Grammar school is attributed to the twelfth century bishop Bjarni and the original Sang school to Earl Rognvald. How accurate these attributions are it is difficult to be sure but bishop Reid can certainly be held responsible for seeing that they were now established on a firm foundation.

Notes

1. Hossack; "Kirkwall in the Orknies" p.64

2. Barbara Crawford: "An Unrecognisable Statue" in "Northern Isles Connections" ed. B. Crawford (Orkney Press)

3. Wallace: "Islands of Orkney" (1700)

4. Richard Fawcett: "Kirkwall Cathedral: an Architectural Analysis" from "St. Magnus Cathedral and Orkney's Twelth Century Renaissance". p.109 ed. Barabara Crawford.

5. Peterkin: "Rentals of Orkney" app. p.18

6. A similar arrangement pertains to this day in St. George's Chapel, Windsor Castle, where retired senior offices from H.M.'s services (known as Military Knights), living in a row of grace and favour houses opposite the chapel, occupy the stalls of the Knights of the Garter on special occasions in the absence of those knights.

7. John Mooney: "The Cathedral and Royal Burgh of Kirkwall". p.49 ff.

5 None

Justitia tua, justitia in aeturnum: et lux tua veritas.

i. Trouble on the border and death of the king

On the 1st of December 1541, after returning from his first visit to Orkney, Reid was expected to leave Edinburgh and join with the bishop of Aberdeen and others in yet another embassy to the king of England, as there was, once again, trouble on the borders in Teviotdale and Lidderdale.

In the sixteenth century an area, as wild and unmapped as the border region of England and Scotland, was in a constant state of undeclared warfare. Property boundaries were illdefined or nonexistent and, as cattle had even less knowledge of them than their owners, cattle rustling was a daily occurrence. Feuds were inevitable and usually bloody. There were times when such border disputes could be used as an excuse for a major campaign by one country or the other. There were also times when neither country could gain by such unrest and would have preferred peace on their borders. It seems that Robert Reid was regarded as a man acceptable to both kingdoms as one able to bring peace, at least temporarily, to the region. It was not the first nor the last time that he was to be involved in border disputes.

On December 3 1541 Sir Thomas Wharton wrote to the Privy Council to inform them that the "Busshopp of Aberdeyn, the lait Abbat of Glenluse (Kinloss) and Thomas Bellynden justices clerke" had been intending to leave Edinburgh on 1st December in order to attend the king (Henry VIII) as ambassadors. The same ambassadors, so his spy informed him, as were at the conclusion of the last peace. The spy also suggested that King James would not himself come to meet Henry for fear of the latter coming north to invade the borders. Meanwhile, on St. Andrew's Day, so he had heard, the Scottish king would be in Edinburgh before departing for the borders, though whether to punish the people of Lidderdale or to go hawking, his spy was unsure!

Sir Thomas concludes his letter with a list of "Slaughters and cruell murdures and doyn within the kinges highnes West Marches of Englond by Scottish men at sundry tymes sithens the begynnyng of the peace, agaynst the trewes"[1]

On the 5th December, James himself wrote to his uncle:

Richt excellent, richt hie and michty prince, oure derrest brother and uncle, we commend ws unto you in oure maist effectuous maner. Signifying that upon oure divers letteris past of befor, we haiil gevin for the encressing of hartlie lufe and favoure with enteir amitie and kyndenes to stand constantlie betuix ws as the proximitie of oure blude requiris, and amoving and putting on syde ony sic thing as apparendlie may hurte or mak impediment thairto, direkkis presentlie towartis you reverend faderis in God, Williame bischop of Abirdene, Robert bischop of Orknay, and Maister Thomas Bellenden, directoure of oure chancellary, oure traist counsalouris and ambassadouris, amply instruct with our mynde, and in likuise for reformatioun of syndri attemptattis laitlie committit on the Bordouris of baith oure realmes, as without gude ordoure and remedie haistelie be put thairto may tend to rupture of the perpetuall peax tane betuix ws be the saidis reverend faderis for oure parte, to grete weill of baith oure realmes and leigis. Prayand you, derrest uncle, to gif ferme and undoubtit credence to oure said ambassadours in all behalvis as unto oure self, and we were with you in propir persoun, as personages singularly gevin for entertenyng of perpetuall peax and conformite of oure mynd to the samyn. Richt excellent, richt hie and michty prince, oure deerest brother and uncle, we pary Eternall God to have you evir in keping. At oure palace of Edinburgh, the fyft day of December, and of oure regnne the xxix yeire (Signed) Your lovyng brother and nepho. James Rex.[2]

On 11th December Sir Cuthbert Radclyff, deputy warden of the Middle Marches, wrote to the Privy Council informing them that since the return of the earlier commission that had been investigating the affairs on the Borders, there had been few incursion into either England or Scotland. The ambassadors from Scotland, "the Busschope of Abberdene, the Buschope of Orknaye and an other temperall man"[3] with forty horsemen, he informed them, had arrived in Alnwick on Saturday night 10th December. He feared that the ambassadors were going to blame him for the retaliation that the English had made for the burning of an English property by the Scots. He wishes the king's majesty to confront the ambassadors with these charges. He would have liked to attend and defend his actions and answer any charges against him and show proof that it was the Scots who always began the trouble, but he dare not leave his post without the king's licence.

He enclosed a long list of charges against the Scots.

Meanwhile the Scottish Ambassadors wrote to the Lord Privy Seal on 15th December advising him of their mission[4]. They apologised for the delay in coming to the king but blame the time of year and 'deipnes of the way'.

They in turn complain that the king of England's subjects have been raiding into Teviotdale and Lidderdale and other places which would have drawn a response had not their king strictly forbidden any retaliation, as he had agreed with his uncle. Any further incursions, they warn, would only cause more trouble which neither king wishes. As a man who loves peace and amity they asked the Lord Privy Seal to request his king to issue 'sharp charges' to the wardens of the Middle and West Marches to see that no further incursions take place during their mission 'undir greit and hie panis'. Their sovereign master has done the same for his wardens, 'sua that nane of the princis liegis on aither of the Borderis be hurt or skathit'.

The embassy arrived in London on 31st December where they received an answer to their complaints but failed to achieve any satisfactory result.

In June the following year Reid and Lord Erskine were again commissioned to treat with the English over the trouble in the Borders. Despite protracted negotiations with many parties they received no satisfaction and further discussions were postponed. It was arranged then that a meeting should take place between James and Henry at York in September of 1542.

James, however, became very suspicious that his uncle intended to kidnap him should he attend, whilst the clergy were fearful that James, who had already flirted with reforming doctrines, might be persuaded to bring the Scottish church in line with the English.

The Scottish ambassador to England left London and joined Reid in York, the pair of them having the unenviable task of explaining to Henry that James had decided not to attend the meeting. The English king was not pleased though Reid and the ambassador swore "on blood, wounds, nails, body and passion of Christ" that they spoke in good faith. Then when the discussions were failing, they "showed themselves as sorrowful men as" the English had ever seen. Despite their protestaion Reid and Lord Erskine were detained by the English and taken with the invading army to Newcastle so that they would not be able to inform their king of the English intentions. The bishop elect of Orkney had, it seems, been made to suffer the fate predicted for King James! Reid succeeded in writing to his sovereign, however, informing him of his situation and ending with the words "lippin, Schir, na uther bot all extremite and weir incontinent".

How Reid managed to escape and return to Edinburgh is not known, although he may well have been released by the English as a valuable go-between whom they had learnt to trust. Seemingly indispensable in this role, when the English army entered Scotland Reid was, in October 1542, sent by the king once more to sue for peace. At the same time James, against the advice and wishes of many of his advisors, was planning an invasion of England with the support of Cardinal Beaton, who had been advocating a crusade against the English.

Reid was accompanied on his peace mission this time by James Learmonth, master of the king's household. They met the duke of Norfolk, Henry's lieutenant general, half a mile from Farneton. The mission was again a failure. The English believed that, despite an earlier setback when a small force had been defeated by the Scots at Haddon Rig, they had the advantage over a divided Scottish command. At Solway Moss this proved to be disastrously the case. Oliver Sinclair, a member of the family of the former earls of Orkney and who had been granted the tack of Orkney and Shetland, led the Scottish army which was put to rout. The news of the defeat sent James into despair. He returned first to Edinburgh, then to the queen at Linlithgow and finally retired to Falkland where he took to his bed.

On 14th December 1542, King James died at the age of thirty years. Although distressed by the military disasters, the death of his two sons and the antagonism of his lords, it is difficult to believe that a young man would have died simply from despair. Depression could perhaps have led to his taking his own life or he may have suffered from one of the many infections which took such a toll in those days. He may even have been poisoned by one of his rebellious lords though this would have been out of character with the times in Scotland where, despite all his failings, a king was still the embodiment of the nation.

James V was evidently not a very likeable man, often vindictive and brutal and politically inept, he made many enemies. Men were not sad to see him go but he left Scotland, once more, with the uncertainties of an infant monarchy and a female one at that.

Robert Reid had been well treated by James and had repaid his king many times over in loyal and devoted service. He would continue to serve his new monarch with the same devotion and ability. It was not however the monarch that he was now called on to serve but the regent, the queen mother, Marie of Guise.

The result of James' death was to leave Scotland once more in a political vacuum. No one was quite sure whether the dying king had made any pronouncement as to who was to assume executive powers during the queen's minority. Various claims were advanced as to what his wishes had been. In the event a council of five members was formed including Cardinal Beaton. For some time the most powerful man in the realm next to the governor had been the Cardinal archbishop of St. Andrew's, David Beaton, Reid's metropolitan. Beaton was a larger than life character. He was undoubtedly very jealous of the church's position and determined to keep the forces of reform at bay. He was however above all a politician and, in his insistence on maintaining the French alliance, he was as much concerned with keeping the English out of Scottish affairs as he was with maintaining the catholic faith. In order to gather around him a strong body of supporters against the 'English party' he saw to it that the bishops who were to be provided by the pope were those on whom he could depend. The bishops in turn were grateful for the presence of such a strong supporter of their rights.

When first appointed to St. Andrew's, Beaton had made Reid, then abbot of Kinloss, one of his vicars-general, a position the archbishop renewed when he left for France in 1541. It was Beaton who saw in Robert Reid the qualities that made him a good negotiator and resulted in Reid's being called upon to serve so often as an ambassador. He was probably also influential in Robert Reid receiving the mitre and the bishop was happy to show his appreciation of the cardinal's friendship. Nevertheless it may have irked him at the number of times in which the cardinal tended to regard him as a useful tool in furthering his own ambitions.

By the following January Arran, who was heir presumptive to the throne, had established himself as sole governor and had quarrelled with the cardinal. The Douglases and other anglophile lords now returned from England. Many of them were openly advocating the adoption of an English style reformation. Under their influence the governor began to show leanings toward protestantism on English lines, though still distrusting heretics. It was, however, only a temporary phase known as "the governor's godly fit" and, as was common with so much of Arran's ideas, it did not last. However, an act introduced by Lord Maxwell for the dissemination of bibles in the vernacular was passed by parliament. After complaints from the church this was restricted to the New Testament only.

Sir George Douglas now proved himself a worthy opponent of the cardinal. It was on his urging that Arran felt able to have the cardinal arrested on 27.January 1543 whilst attending council, accusing Beaton of inviting French intervention in Scotland. Although siding with Sir George, the governor must have known that the grounds for Beaton's imprisonment were weak, and attempts to dispose of the cardinal were to be short lived.

ii. The bishop and the cardinal

The English king was intent on arranging a marriage between the Scottish queen and his son and heir, Prince Edward. The governor urged on by the 'English party' were prepared to agree. Peace was sought with Henry VIII and once again a safe conduct was requested for the bishop of Orkney, to be the Scottish ambassador to treat for it. In the event Reid's involvement was not required, so he retired for a time to his abbey at Kinloss.

Whether Reid's presence would have made any difference in the negotiations that produced the Treaty of Greenwich, it is hard to say. He would surely have been reluctant to be part of any arrangement for Mary to marry the English king's son, knowing, as he would have done, that it could not possibly have had the cardinal's approval. It may be that he made his opinion clear on the matter which was why his services were dispensed with. In any event parliament soon made it apparent that they were unhappy with the settlement and that they still acknowledged Arran's claim to the succession in the event of Mary failing to produce an heir. Even the Douglases, anxious about their reinstatement, soon became less enthusiastic about Henry's claims.

With the reluctance of the Scottish nobles to accept his son as a future husband to the queen of Scotland, Henry began his harrasment of the borders that came to be known as the 'Rough wooing'.

It was not long before Robert Reid, bishop of Orkney, was to find himself once more concerned with the archbishop's affairs. Although closely associated with the cardinal he was trusted on all sides as an honest and incorruptable mediator. In the spring of 1543 he went south again to visit Beaton in St, Andrew's where the cardinal was then in confinement, after periods at Dalkeith, Seton and Blackness.

Back in St. Andrew's in his own archbishopric, Beaton had found himself at much greater liberty. A convention at Perth of many earls, bishops, abbots, barons and knights entrusted the bishop of Orkney with the task of carrying their demands to the Governor that 1. The Cardinal be put at liberty. 2. The new testament should not "go abroad". 3. The

Governor should be counselled by them and 4. the ambassadors whom Henry VIII had requested should not be sent but others, nominated by themselves, should be sent instead.

The Governor refused and summoned parliament. Meanwhile the Cardinal, ever since his return to St. Andrew's, had been acquiring increasing freedom of action and by Easter he was able to celebrate Mass in the cathedral so that his imprisonment was virtually at an end. Robert Reid was now firmly committed to the Cardinal, yet, elected to be lord of the articles in parliament, he was appointed to the governor's privy council. He was the one man who was indispensable to both parties, who could be trusted to exercise a degree of impartiality rare among the feuding nobles at the time.

The cardinal was still reluctant to leave his home base of St. Andrew's and go to Edinburgh. From St. Andrew's he sent the bishop of Orkney to Sir Ralph Sadler, the English ambassador, to request a meeting. Beaton expressed the fear that should he go himself to Sadler he might be "entrapped" but that should the ambassador go to him at St. Andrew's, Sadler "should have good cause" to think his journey "well bestowed." Sadler replied to Reid, as he had already done to the cardinal's chaplain, that he was uncertain of the cardinal's standing with the governor. Reid then prayed Sadler to advise his master that "the cardinal was much addicted to your majesty, and was the sorrowfulest man alive to hear that your majesty was displeased with him, which he protested was without cause, as he was able to prove, whatsoever information was made to your grace against him: And if he might come frankly to this council without danger, to say his opinion in those great matters, for the common weal of this realm, he would declare himself of good zeal to bring all your reasonable desires to good pass, and labour as well, and as effectually in the same, as any man alive".[5] Sadler was clearly not to be persuaded and declined to speak to the cardinal unless Beaton appeared at court and he was unable to avoid him. He was obviously uncertain as to the cardinal's future standing at court despite the latter's protestations and preferred to wait upon events. He assured his king however that within two days it should be evident "what is to be trusted to and looked for at their hands".[5]

Despite his fine words, once free the cardinal, with his supporters, rose against the governor's policy of appeasement of the English. Reid was delegated to meet the governor's commissioners at Winchburgh to represent the cardinal's views. He was to persuade the governor to join with the cardinal's party in a bond of mutual defence "under the Umber of the Queen's authority". Reid returned to tell Beaton that the governor was now 'well-minded' toward him but would not agree to holding the convention at Stirling. He required the cardinal to come to Edinburgh. The cardinal however was not so easily reassured and Reid, together with Lord Fleming was sent back to obtain pledges for his security. Beaton further required that the castle of Edinburgh should be delivered by the governor into the care of the provost of the town and all weapons that had been removed therefrom to be restored. Foot soldiers mustered by the governer should be disbanded. The citizens of Leith, which citizens were believed to in favour of reform, should be barred from leaving home and coming to Edinburgh during the convention, and "the councils should be kept in the town, in their judicial house, called the Tolbooth". Finally that the governor should attend without any about him bearing arms.

The governor declined to give such assurances, although he was prepared to pledge his own son that they could come and go safely and that Sir George Douglas, and any others of whom they might be afraid, would do likewise. In July 1543 the cardinal decided that it would be a blow to Arran's prestige at the time of the ratification of the treaties with England if the queen and her mother could be removed from his influence. A large force descended upon Linlithgow castle only to find it had been well fortified and access to the queen was impossible.

The cardinal then gathered together a large company of lords and clerics who signed a bond to defend the realm and protect the queen in the face of the English king's plans. The bond in addition opposed ecclesiastical reform. The clerics were therefore happy to give their support and Bishop Robert Reid was among the signataries.

The cardinal still declined to attend the ratification of the treaties and appointed bishop Reid in his place as one of the representatives to examine the treaties with the governor's commissioners. This Reid did and was present when they were signed with due ceremony in Edinburgh on 25th August.

At the same time he and the cardinal had privately agreed the proposed marriage of the queen with the governor's son, in preference to the proposed wedding to the English prince. Despite this, as a member of the council to direct the governor, he, along with other members, sent for the English ambassador to discuss peace and the royal marriage. The governor meanwhile continued to abide by the treaty which agreed the marriage of Prince Edward to Queen Mary whilst informing the English ambassador of the plan, that Reid and the cardinal had agreed, for the

St. Magnus Cathedral and ruins of Bishop's Palace from a 19th century engraving. The scene would have been similar to that of the 16th century although the palace was then under construction or complete.

St. Magnus Cathedral today.

Ruins of Abbots Tower at Kinloss Monastery.

Ruins of Kinloss Abbey.

The Interior of St. Magnus Cathedral

**Ruins of Bishop's Palace
in Kirkwall.**

**Doorway to the south side of
the Cathedral, attributed to Robert Reid**

**Bishop Reid's Bookplate stamped on
the covers of all his books**
Courtesy of University of St. Andrews Library,
Dept. of Manuscripts and Muniments

**Chapel of Immaculate Conception (previously St. Andrew) in the church of St. Jacques, Dieppe.
Probable burial place of Reid and his fellow commissioners.**

queen to marry his own son. No doubt he was seeking to stir up still further Henry's antagonism to the cardinal.

A safe conduct for Reid and another councillor to meet with Henry was requested but, not surprisingly, refused.

The bishop continued to act in his legal capacity as a justice of the college and in 1543 was one of the arbitrators between William, lord Crichton of Sanquhar and Mr. John Leslie, parson of Kinnoul, in an action concerning the parsonage.

iii. Perth heresy trial

The town of Perth at this time was becoming a thorn in the side of the Cardinal as a place where the reformers were making many converts. Beaton therefore decided to make an example of some of its citizens in the hope that 'heresy' there might be stamped out. Since he had been refused a safe conduct to England, Reid was free to attend to his legal duties and joined the governor and the cardinal at Perth on 25th January 1544. Many of the citizens were believed to be guilty of heresy but only a handful were picked out for trial, Robert Lamb, a merchant; William Anderson, maltman; James Hunter, a flesher; James Ronaldson, a skinner, and his wife Helen Stirk and James Finlayson. Lamb was accused of interrupting and contradicting a friar when preaching and, with Anderson and Ronaldson, of 'hanging up the image of St. Francis on a cord, nailing a ramme's hornes to his head, and a kowe's rumpe to his taile; and for eating of a goose on Allhallow even" (Calderwood)[6]. James Hunter was simply charged with being in the company of the other accused. Helen Stirk was accused of refusing to call on the Virgin Mary during childbirth but only on God, thereby implying that the Virgin had no merit despite her being chosen as the mother of God. James Ronaldson had particularly offended the cardinal having 'set upon the round of his fourth staire the three-crowned diademe of Peter, carved of tree'. This the cardinal believed to have been made in mockery of himself! They were duly convicted and executed as an example to others. The church, of course, could not pronounce the death penalty nor carry it out. For this they were handed over to the civil authorities. It was the reverse of Pilate's action in handing Jesus over to the priests!

The sentences may seem a harsh, especially in view of what would seem to have been very trivial offences, but it was no more than was prescribed by statute once the charge of heresy had 'proved' Here 'proof' would seem to have been a matter of of expediency rather than of justice. What must clearly be in question was whether the charges ever really amounted to heresy or whether these poor, and no doubt ignorant, folk were simply being made scapegoats to put the fear of God, or rather that of the cardinal, into the citizens of Perth. Despite the severity meeted out on this occasion, in most other cases every opportunity was given to heretics to recant and receive a lesser sentence of escheat of goods or banishment. Many took advantage of such opportunities. Persistence in the heresy could, in law, be attended by only one sentence. Reid, like the rest of the judges, was caught up in the code and practice of the times. Despite his evident humanity it is probably that he did so without qualms. It was a cruel age but at least in Scotland, apart from some of the excesses of James V, it was less cruel than in England where hanging, drawing and quartering were commonplace and regarded as barbaric by the Scots.

iv. Reid as peacemaker once more

At the beginning of 1544, before the Perth heresy trial, the Cardinal and the Governor had attempted to bring about an agreement between themselves and the opposition led by Angus and Lennox. In effect it was to require the latter to admit their faults and obtain forgiveness. Beaton wrote to the Queen Mother that 'The lords beand met at Leith, are agreant with My Lord Governor and was contentit to summit thame to the ordinance and decrete of my lordis of Agile, Murray, Bischop of Orkney, My Lord Sanct John, the Knycht of Caldour and Hew Campbell of Lowden... Quha have devisit the matter and gevin in thair deliverance as followis: that is to say that all thir lordis of the Westland beand in Leith and thair followeris sall have fre remissioun of all faltis and crymes bygane: and all thingis quhairin at thai ar hurt or skaithit sall be dressit at the sycht of the Lordis forsaidis, and that thai ar to have na mair ado with Ingland.'[7]

The opposition refused to commit themselves without a meeting with the Cardinal, Argyll, Moray and the bishop of Orkney. Robert Reid was again put in the position of peace maker and met the rebel lords on 13th January 1544 at the rood chapel of Greenside between Edinburgh and Leith where they eventually agreed to the cardinals terms. The following day the bishop and cardinal rode together to Greenside and brought the rebels back to the governor's lodgings in Edinburgh where "perfect concord" was ensured. On the 17th January, Reid convened a meeting with the earl of Angus in Edinburgh to settle all outstanding quarrels with the governor and to ensure the latter's future safety.

As so often happened between the contending parties at this time the bishop's hard work in achieving a reconciliation was short lived, Lennox and the Douglases soon breaking the agreement. In March Reid went to the earl of Angus, in order to attempt to reconcile him with the governor and in the following month persuaded the governor to release Adam Otterburn who had been detained. As a result of Reid's peacemaking efforts the Cardinal arrogantly wrote to Henry VIII to to suggest that his Scottish friends had now deserted him and requesting a safe conduct for Scottish envoys to discuss the re-establishment of peace. Henry returned a stinging reply. He wrote back telling the Cardinal that, if he intended to meddle in affairs of the world instead of keeping to his office as a minister of the gospel, which he professed to do when made bishop, he should have better regard for the "honour and weale" of the realm than he had had so far and, if he wanted an answer to his request for a safe conduct for ambassadors his, Henry's, reply would be directed to the council by the Ross herald and the cardinal could hear it there.

In June 1544 Reid found himself obliged to act in opposition to the cardinal to whom he had previously given all his support. The Queen Dowager held a convention in Stirling which demanded the suspension of the governor. At the urging of the cardinal the governor had agreed to abandon the treaties with England. Reid who had been a party to their ratification felt bound to support the Queen Dowager in this matter. Parliament however was the only body which could legally dismiss the governor and with the reconciliation between cardinal and governor the Queen Dowager's bid for power could not be maintained.

However in September a council was formed with the queen-dowager at its head. It was to consist of the cardinal, the earls of Huntly, Moray, Lennox, Angus, Argyle, Bothwell and Maricshal, the archbishop of Glasgow, the chancellor, and the bishops of Moray, Orkney, Galloway and Dunblane and the abbots of Paisley and Coupar. They were to advise and direct the governor. Lord Fleming and the abbot of Paisley were deputed to persuade Angus and the rest of the 'English' party to join.

No doubt thankful to be free for a time from the political manoeuveres and petty squabbles of the temporal lords, in September 1544 Reid was at last able to return to the spiritual domain of his island diocese. As has already been recorded, now was the time when he completed the reform of the cathedral chapter and the architectural improvements that he had put in train.

Meanwhile back in Edinburgh John Maxwell of Dunray, who was said to owe a large sum to the bishop of Orkney, was appealing to the Archbishop of St. Andrew's, against the bishop's claim. He had previously obtained exemption from the governor from appearing before the bishop himself, or his chapter, or any other judge other than the archbishop. The official of Orkney appeared on behalf of bishop Reid. Maxwell also brought complaints concerning the profits of Burray and the teinds of Stronsay. In the event both cases were suspended by the lords of council and were quashed by the official of St. Andrews as unreasonable. Maxwell was required to pay costs.

v. A clan battle and an ecclesiastical one

There is a tradition among the Fraser family that Robert Reid, at this time, was tutor to Alexander, the young Lord Lovat.

Alexander's father and elder brother had both been killed in 1544 at the battle of Lochy, the last great clan battle to be fought on Scottish soil. It was fought over a claim to the Clanranald estates. Ranald. a nephew and foster child of the Lovats, had his claim challenged by the bastard son of his elder brother and a force of highlanders invaded the Lovat lands in the latter's support. The Earl of Huntly came to the aid of the Lovats but their forces became divided and in a battle at the head of Loch Lochy the Frasers were defeated amidst great slaughter on both sides.

The bishop since becoming Commendator of Beauly, had always had a close association with the Lovats and it is probably true that he had taken an interest in the younger Fraser since his childhood. Knowing how keen he was on the education of the young it is also probable that he did indeed oversee the young man's education. There is some uncertainty as to Alexander's age at the time his father died. He is said by some to have been seventeen but it is more likely that he was, in fact, only seven. He may have been attached to his tutor but the story that, on hearing of the bishop's death he exclaimed "Would God I were with thee, my dear father, Robert Reid, my patron, my pattern, my priest, my bishop. Alas I will never see him, he will never return" is clearly apocryphal since Alexander died a year before the bishop!

Now, once again, Reid's services as ambassador were called upon in May of 1545 and a safe conduct was requested for him to wait upon Henry VIII. Presumably the safe conduct was refused for he never went, which, considering the treatment he had received on his earlier embassy was perhaps just as well.

Having failed to obtain safe conduct to bargain for peace with the English, the bishop of Orkney's services as an ambassador were no longer required for the next four years, as the war with England continued. Thus he was enabled to concentrate on matters nearer home and was able to take his seat in the privy council. There Reid agreed that everything possible should be done to protect the realm when there was an offer by the French to send troops to help defend Scotland or to launch an attack on the English. Among the duties he was called on to perform during these years was as receiver of accounts of the chamberlain of the priory of St. Andrew's in October 1545.

It is a sad reflection on the state of the catholic church in Scotland at this time, and one that must have done much to encourage the reformers, that the two most powerful churchmen in the land were bitter rivals and showed no hesitation in demonstrating the fact.

When the Cardinal's uncle, James Beaton, had been translated to the see of St. Andrew's in 1523 he was succeeded in 1524, as archbishop of Glasgow, by Gavin Dunbar. The two prelates were frequently in dispute over precedence. The Archbishop of Glasgow had obtained, from the Pope, exemption from the jurisdiction of the primatial see of St. Andrew's. In 1535, on a visit to Dumfries, James Beaton - possibly encouraged by his nephew David, then abbot of Arbroath and keeper of the royal seal - had his cross born before him and publicly blessed the people. To this the Archbishop of Glasgow objected strongly. Then in 1539 the representatives of David Beaton, now archbishop of St. Andrew's and recently made cardinal, was present at a heresy trial in Glasgow presided over by Dunbar. The cardinal's representative disagreed with the archbishop of Glasgow's leniency and reminded him that he should agree with the cardinal's policy in such matters. Neither event served to soften Gavin Dunbar's feelings toward his fellow archbishop. Beaton requested, but failed to obtain from the Pope, the cancellation of Glasgow's exemption from the jurisdiction of the St. Andrew's see. Neither could he obtain papal sanction to have his cross borne before him in the Glasgow diocese. Nevertheless Beaton went ahead and once again, in Dumfries, had the Archbishop of St. Andrew's cross carried in public, thereby ensuring further protests from the Glasgow diocesan authorities. In 1544

Archbishop Dunbar was among those who sought to suspend the governor, largely as a means of depriving Beaton of his influence. In 1544 the Pope appointed Beaton *legate a latere* in Scotland, thereby giving him extensive powers over all ecclesiastical affairs. To Dunbar, who had been archbishop when Beaton was yet to be made abbot of Arbroath, this must have been a bitter blow. Beaton did not hesitate to demonstrate the authority that his new position afforded him and on Palm Sunday he attempted to have his cross carried publicly in Glasgow itself, resulting in the usual protest. Far from exhibiting a spirit of christian humility and fellowship in keeping with their calling, the two prelates presented a picture of petty pride that can only have lowered them in the esteem of the faithful.

Then in 1545 matters came to a head when a second attempt was made to carry the Cardinal's cross in Glasgow. The attendants of the respective archbishops thereupon took it upon themselves to defend their respective masters' privileges. John Knox gives a vivid description, in his 'History'[8], of what ensued:

"Coming forth (or going in, all is one) at the choir door of Glasgow Kirk, begins striving for state betwixt the two cross-bearers, so that from glowming they come to shouldering; from shouldering they go to buffets and from dry blows, by neffs (fists) to neffling; and then for charity's sake they cry, 'Dispersit dedit pauperibus' and essays which of the crosses is finest metal, which staff was strongest, and which bearer could best defend his master's pre-eminence; and that there should be no superiority in that behalf, to the ground go both the crosses. And then began no little fray, but yet a merry game; for rochets were rent, tippets were torn, crowns were knapped, and side gowns might have been seen wantonly to wag from one wall to the other... But the sanctuary we suppose, saved the lives of many. How merrily that ever this be written, it was bitter bourding (jesting) to the Cardinal and his court... and yet the other (Dunbar) in his folly, as proud as a peacock, would let the cardinal know that he was a bishop when the other was but Beaton, before he got Arbroath".

Such a public brawl between the factions of the two leading churchmen, though no doubt entertaining to the citizens of Glasgow, must have left them wondering at a church that put a higher priority on the status of its servants than on the dignity of their office and the purpose of their mission.

Although the bishop of Orkney was a suffragan of the archbishop of St. Andrew's and no doubt owed much to the the Cardinal, he was one of very few who could be trusted by both sides to be sufficiently impartial to undertake the investigation of witnesses to the affair. He did so, made his dispositions and, at the request of the governor, sent his report to the Pope to provide the remedy.

vi. Death of the cardinal

On the 24th May 1546 Reid had his last meeting with his archbishop. The Governor and the Cardinal met a small gathering of councillors, Andrew and George Durie, the Cardinal's cousins; the abbot of Paisley, the Governor's brother; and two bishops, William Chisholm of Dunblane and Robert Reid of Orkney. The only business appears to have been to order the justice clerk to enforce the acts against those of the Merse and Teviotdale 'that sittis undir assurance of England'.

Four days later on the 28th May 1546 a conspiracy, that had been forming against the Cardinal ever since the burning for heresy of the popular preacher George Wishart, came to a head. The Cardinal was assassinated in his own castle by three of the conspirators, well paid, it is said, for their efforts, by the English.

Following the assassination the council was reformed with four lords being chosen as a secret council to remain with the governor. One of the four, in June 1546 and again in March 1547, was the bishop of Orkney. He was also kept busy in Parliament, in auditing the accounts of the lord high treasurer and as curator to the Earl of Athol.

The death of Cardinal Beaton meant that the archbishopric of St. Andrew's had become vacant. Robert Reid, by any criterion, was the most fitted to have succeeded to the see. However he lacked the qualification of being the governor's "lecherous bastard brother". Instead he had to content himself with delivering the pallium, as papal mandatory, to James Hamilton. By the same token he also failed to measure up to the qualifications required for the archbishopric of Glasgow which had also fallen vacant. He was not of the nobility and the post went to a Gordon who was replaced as abbot by a ten year old son of the governor!

The governor's privy council, of which the bishop of Orkney was a member, agreed that bills, concerning the administration of justice in civil causes, should be dealt with by the lords in session and not by the privy council. They also discharged the lords who were the queen's guardians.

Robert Reid was given the responsibility of finding a competent doctor to attend the queen and is believed to have been responsible for tutoring the young queen in religion. Although there is no contemporary evidence for the latter, the bishop's reputation as an educator and his known closeness to the queen would undoubtedly have fit him for the task. It may be that it was the influence of Robert Reid that bred in Mary, when she eventually took over the reins of government, the tolerance that allowed her to rule her protestant subjects whilst remaining true to the faith of her forbears.

vii. President of the Court of Justice

Robert Reid continued to adjudicate in several private affairs, such as being advisor to the countess of Huntly and her son, Lord Gordon. On 7 March 1548 he also arbitrated in respect of a sasine in favour of Katherine Dunbrek, widow of David Peirsounde of the lands of Weland in Shapinsay, and of the lands of Ourquy in Evie, her kinsman, John Dunbrek, acting on her behalf.

At the start of 1549 Reid succeeded to the presidency of the College of Justice, the supreme court of the land, on the death, the previous year, of abbot Myln. His skill as a lawyer had brought him to the pinnacle of the legal profession and he lost no time in making his presence felt.

Professor Hannay[9] writing about the College of Justice says that 'Early in that year (1549) the privy council found itself so much beset by petitioners, whose business the College of Justice had been created to deal, that it ordained the prelates "to se the lordis of sessioun payit thar yeirlie pensionis" and that the lords themselves "to sit continewalie... in all sic actionis as hes bene in tymes bypast discussit in the sessioun" doing justice to all parties as they would answer to God.'

One of the new President's first acts was to 'register an act of sederunt regulating the allocation of salaries, hitherto loose and unsatisfactory. Henceforth remuneratuion should be "eftir the rait of thar residence be quotidiane dsiributioun conforme to the bull of erection." If collectors handed sums to individual judges without awaiting annual accounts, there would be no allowances made upon audit, while the recipients were to be fined in double the amount; and the clerks of court were directed to take particular note of attendances from day to day. Meanwhile the factors had gathered up arrears to the extent of over £2300. No reckoning had been heard "thir mony yeirs bigane." After some controversy, due to the fact that the necessary calculations went back even to the days of James V, the money was allotted at the rate of £40 for each year of service, so as to clear the ground and make a fresh start according to the terms of the papal foundation.'

Despite these regulation the College still failed to raise the amount for any one year, many of the contributors defaulting. Whilst Myln was President he was paid from royal funds a larger salary than his colleagues in recognition of his presidential responsibilities. Reid, however, was considered to be adequately remunerated by virtue of his holding both the bishopric of Orkney and the monastic houses of Kinloss and Beauly, and remunerated only by having his own quota of the subsidy, amounting to £36, remitted to him.

In addition to the continuing arrears in contributions to the running of the College, the record of attendances by a number of the lords was regrettably low. Of 973 individual attendances, 925 were accounted for by a mere eight of the fourteen lords.

Late in 1549 the bishop was back in his diocese. Whilst there he agreed the Assedation of Skokness to his friend Edward Sinclair of Strome:

"Be it kend tyllall men be yr present Letters, us Robet, be the mercie of God bischope of Orknay, That forasmeikle as ane honourable man, Edwarde Sinclair of Strome, has shawin in deed his faytful kyndness and tane a trew part with us and our friendis, and spedlie in the defenss of Chrysten fayt and liberie of haly kirk at our being now in our diocye of Orknay, and is oblist to do ye samen in tymes cuming and to help fortifie and supple our friendis bayt in spiritual and temporale juisdictioun, and not to let us or them be wrangit sa fer as he may of ressoun: Thairfor to have sett and for male letten, and ye tennor heirof settis, and for male lettis to the said Edwarde, and to Margaret Dishingtoun, his spous, and to the langest levar of yame twa, and yair subtennentis, and ortua, all and Haill our Landis of Skowkness, in Rousay, with ye myln and holme of the samyn with yair pertientis... Payand heirfor... ane barrell butter at the custimat tme of yeir... In witness hereof to this our assedatioun, subscrunt wt. our hand, our signet is affixt at Kirkwall the xxvi. day of October, the yeir of God jm. vc. xlix. yeirs." Kirkwall he helped, "with his spiritual and temporal jurisdiction".[10]

Edward Sinclair was to remain a staunch catholic after the Reformation and would not "thole that the mass were done".

Reid's visit to Kirkwall was once again only a brief one for he had returned to Edinburgh by November to attend the synod and provincial council of the ordinaries, prelates and other clergy held at the Blackfriars' Church. The reform of the clergy's morals was one of the chief subjects. Mindful of his own diocese at the council, the bishop of Orkney managed to obtain a perpetual sustentation for preachers who became provosts of Kirkwall, thereby benefiting his old college friend, Malcolm Halcro!

viii. The trial of Adam Wallace. [11]

The provincial council also saw to it that the death of the Cardinal did not put an end to the church's pursuit of heretics. In 1550 Adam Wallace was brought to trial at the Blackfriars' church. Along with the archbishop of St. Andrew's and other prelates and lords, the bishop of Orkney took his place to hear the charges.

"It is an horrible heresie!" said the Bishop of Orkney.

Poor Adam Wallace had just propounded the protestant objection to the doctrine of transubstantiation, the belief that the bread and wine of the communion actually turned into the flesh and blood of Christ at the eucharist. The bishop wished to hear no more. 'Ad secundum' was the cry. Guilt on the first count had become self-evident, and the court passed on to hear the second indictment against the accused.

What sort of a man was this that was so horrified by the denial of a doctrine that most today find hard to accept as credible. He was a man of his time, both learned and deeply spiritual. To such a man the teachings of the church were not to be lightly contested, especially by a man whose learning and intellect fell short of his own, a man who was prepared to place his own reading and interpretation of scriptures above that of centuries of divines. At the Last Supper, Jesus said, 'This is my body which is broken for you... this is my blood of the new testament which is shed for you and for many...'. What right had ignorant men to deny the words of the Christ?

"It is the Spirit that quickeneth;" Wallace had said,"The flesh profiteth nothing to be eaten, as they took it, and even so ye take it." Such sentiments went to very heart of the church's teachings, it denied one of the foundation stones on which the church was built. Christ had given his body on the cross and the bread and wine were that body and blood alive again for the sustenance of the faithful. It was not a trivial matter.

Adam Wallace was condemned to death for his heresy. At his execution the Earl of Glencairn turned to the Bishop of Orkney and others and said:"I take you all, my lords of the clergy here present, to witness that I here protest for my part, that I consent not to his death". There is no report that the Bishop disagreed with the Earl nor condemned him for his sentiments. However he did presumably accede to the sentence. It is likely that he attended the burning of heretics on at least two occasions. Today this would appear to many the actions of a cruel and vindictive man. But Reid did not live today. In another five hundred years our descendants may marvel at the inhumanity we display in locking men up in prisons that can be universities of crime to learn the very arts they are being punished for committing. In the absence of antibiotics cautery has always been regarded as an effective method of sterilising a wound. Just so was burning considered a way of cauterising a damaged soul and the man at the stake was given the chance of having his heresy burned out of him. The trouble was that heresy was too often regarded as an means of political correction when the state used it as an excuse for eliminating its enemies. Despite his high office in the judiciary and the queen's council, it is unlikely that Reid would have abused his office in this respect.

One of the greatest tragedies of the age was that men could kill and could lay down their lives for their personal interpretations of the same faith. It is a tragedy, alas, that still infects part of our own age. Nevertheless the very extremes to which men would go to uphold their convictions was a measure of the hold that faith had upon them. The abandonment of such convictions, though admitting a greater tolerance, has too often meant the abandonment of fundamental principles. Measures, however well meant, to achieve reconciliation may, therefore, involve a loss of faith itself. Somehow men need to learn to allow others their convictions whilst still adhering to their own. No-one has a monopoly of truth but to abandon beliefs for the sake of unity is too often to abandon belief - and thereby to achieve a unity that is worthless. The sixteenth century was often a cruel age but it was an age which believed passionately in the spiritual worth of mankind.

How many other trials of heretics Reid attended is not recorded but it is unlikely to have been many where the death penalty was involved. Although there are records of between one hundred and fifty and two hundred adherents to the protestant cause, and there were no doubt many more that went unrecorded, only fifteen were ever executed for heresy. Of the others some recanted, some suffered escheat of their goods and many left the country for England or the continent. One, William Johnston, an advocate, fled the country and Robert Reid acquired his house for a 'small summe'. When Johnstone returned in the time of Governor Hamilton, he was considered fortunate to have been allowed the use of one room. Presumably this was thought to have been magnanimous on the part of the bishop!

The pursuit of heretics does not, perhaps, place Reid in a particularly good light in our eyes today. Nevertheless he was regarded by his contemporaries as being strict but merciful and certainly by the light of the times and his own convictions he must have regarded his actions in such cases as justifiable.

ix. Legal affairs and embassy to Edward VI

After the English suffered a defeat at Broughty Craig Castle in 1550, Reid, as President of the College of Justice, ordered that customs officers should ensure that foreigners did not carry their money abroad but spent it on Scottish merchandise, in order to prevent much needed gold and silver leaving the country.

Many such legal and fiscal matter now occupied Reid during September 1550. He was procurator for John Groat; testamentary tutor for Katherine and Margaret, daughters of the late Thomas Dunbrek of that ilk; papal mandatory to induct the provost of Tain into the abbacy of the monastery of Fearn; auditor of the accounts of the lord high treasurer; made a contract with John Stewart of Mynto and accordingly paid 500 merks to Charles Dunlop, chaplain, for the redemption of a tenement in Liberton Wynd, Edinburgh.

Toward the end of the year he returned to his diocese once more. To Barbara Stewart of Burray, Margaret Sinclair, her daughter and her future husband, James Tulloch, he leased the islands of Burray, Flotta, Swona, Switha, Glimsholm and Hunda with the teinds of sheaves, for a period of nineteen years. No doubt during this visit he was able to observe what progress had been made on his building projects and assess the success of his appointments to the chapter.

On his return to the mainland of Scotland in the spring of 1551 Bishop Reid was commissioned by the commissary general of Glasgow to hold ordinations in the abbey of Jedburgh and to promote an acolyte of the Dunblane diocese, William Blackwood, to the subdiaconate. Blackwood remained a staunch catholic after the Reformation and was hunted to the end of the century for his 'popery'. It could be that he was a relation of the bishop by marriage as Reid's sister, Helen, married a Blackwood.

Reid continued to be called upon to settle a variety of land ownership disputes. In July 1551 there was one concerning various members of the

Johnstone family. In February 1552 he was arbitrator between James Ogilvie of Balfour and his mother and Mr. George Blair. Later that year, as vicar general of the bishop of Aberdeen, he received the resignation of the lands of Larquhy and Petterfay by John Innes and granted them to John, earl of Athol, in excambion for the lands of Auchluncart. The same year he was appointed commissioner and auditor of the exchequer and auditor of the accounts of the lord high treasurer.

In September 1552 John Hamilton, third son of the duke of Chatelherault, was appointed abbot of Arbroath, and the bishop of Orkney, as papal mandatory, administered the oath to the new abbot. Later in that month he requested that a Mr. Robert Glen be admitted burgess and guild-brother of Edinburgh free of charge.

Later the same year Reid was once more required to use his skills as a negotiator in an embassy to treat with the English. The envoy of the French king, Louis de S.Gelais, sieur de Lansac, had arrived in Scotland from England and with the French ambassador, Henri de Cleutin, seigneur d'Oysel, met the master of Erskine and the bishops of Orkney and Ross who had been appointed Scottish commissioners. The bishop of Ross was later dropped and Robert Reid was deputed to talk with the young English king, Edward VI. He might well have found it a relief to deal with a young and inexperienced prince after his previous dealings with the ageing and wily Henry VIII. The commissioners met the English at Norham where a treaty was concluded. It was agreed to get soldiers withdrawn from the borders and the frontier to remain as before the war; for the English to keep Berwick but give up Roxburgh, Eyemouth and Edrington; the fishing and the debatable lands to remain neutral and no trees to be felled thereon; hostages to be surrendered and prisoners freed; malefactors, murderers and fugitives to be delivered up; sailors and boats to be restored and, if blown into rival ports the sailors to return home and their boats retained. Robert Carnegie of Kinnaird for Scotland and Sir Thomas Chalonner for England ratified the treaty on 14th August 1551.

In 1552 the bishop was named one of the commissioners for the division of Debatable lands by the queen and Governor, but his name was dropped when the English complained that there were too many Scottish commissioners.

However in 1553 the French ambassador in London named the bishop as one of the Scottish commissioner to redress the slaughter and other crimes on the borders, provided the English also agreed to appoint commissioners.

The following Privy Council minute for the 8 September 1553 bears this out[12];

Item inn caise the Quene and Counsale of Inglande condiscend to aggre two said Commisioneris to the Bordouris; desyr the Ambassatour too knaw the namys of thame sall cum for the part of Inglande; that is to say, for Bychopis Murray, Dunblane, Orknay; for Erlis Marschell, Rothes and Cassillis; Knychtis Sir William Hamiltoun of Sanquhair, Jhone Maxwell of Tarreglis, Matelande of Lethyngtoun, Andro Jhonestoun of Elphinstoun, Robert Carnegye of Kynnarde, mr. Jhone Ballenden of Auchtknowle, Maister James McGill of Balgawys, Master David Borthuik of Lochill; sua that sa mony as thai sall caus cum doun for the part of Inglande of semblabull estait.

x. A friend in need and a new abbot of Kinloss

Robert Reid was never slow to help a friend in need. One such friend was Donald McKay of Far who died at about this time leaving no legitimate heir. Since Donald was himself a bastard his property was escheat and passed into the hands of the queen - effectively this was into the hands of the governor. Consent was given to Donald's bastard son, Y McKay, to receive his father's lands on payment of 4000 merks. This was beyond Y's means and, in the event of his failing to pay, the lands were to pass to the bishop of Orkney. The queen then granted the barony of Far with other named lands to the bishop together with the fishing rights for salmon on the river Far and the waters of the Strathy and presented to him the tenancy of all the escheated Mckay lands in Sutherland, Caithness and the sheriffdom of Inverness. The bishop also received part of the lands of Langewall which McKay had held for payment for two chaplains at St. Michael's altar in Moray cathedral.

On the 29th September 1551 Robert Reid made an agreement with Y's curator that, if the young man would pay 1,000 merks, he would resign to him the barony of Durness and, on payment of a second one thousand merks, he would resign to him Strathnaver. On payment of the remaining 2000 merks the rest of the property of Far and other lands would all pass to Y McKay. Meanwhile the bishop paid the 4000 merks demanded by the crown in two instalments of 2000 merks, whilst retaining the revenue from the lands until the full amount was paid by McKay.

However in February of 1553 Y McKay fell foul of the law and on his being declared fugitive and put to the horn for murder, the bishop received the gift of escheat of all his goods. In 1555 when it came to obtaining warrant for his claim however,the bishop was to have trouble with the lords.

Reid's heir, Walter, the son of his brother, James, later sold the rights of Strathnaver to Sir Robert Gordon on behalf of the Earl of Sutherland and it later passed to the earl's son and Sir Donald Mackay. By 1561 Y McKay appears to have regained possession of the lands of Skaill and Regaboill together with the vicarage of Durness (he had, presumably, managed to establish his innocence of the murder charge!). Strathnaver, however, and most of the remaining property was never redeemed, so that Reid and, eventually his estate, was the poorer for most, if not all, of the 4000 merks. This was to have a considerable bearing when it came to satisfying the provisions of the bishop's will.

Another whom Reid was prepared to help financially was the commendator of Coldingham, Lord John Stewart. It will be recalled that this natural son of James V was in receipt of a pension of 800 merks from the bishop, a condition imposed on Reid on his appointment to the see of Orkney. Unfortunately Stewart found himself in financial difficulties. His abbey of Coldingham paid a yearly pension of 400 merks to John Maxwell, a cleric of Glasgow. When Maxwell became Sir John Maxwell of Terregles he assigned the pension to John Bris, vicar of Dumfries. In order to liquidate the pension to Bris, Stewart would be required to find the sum of 1400 merks. This he was quite unable to do. The bishop of Orkney generously agreed to pay the full 1400 merks and reduce the pension to Stewart from 800 merks to 200.

Also in 1552 Bishop Robert was "lord compositor" for the remission to John Nevin in Cunninghamhead and three other persons in the bailiary of Cunningham and two others in the bailie of Kyle for their absence from the army and other crimes.

In the spring of 1553, whether it was his own choice or at the request of the crown, Robert Reid resigned the monastery of Kinloss to a successor. On the 6th April therefore Walter Reid, the bishop's nephew, received the obedience of the monks and on the 16th was solemnly blessed by the bishop in the presence of the Lairds of Innes, Duffus, Walterton, Ochterellane and many other lords. It is uncertain as to whether he also received the commendatorship of Beauly at this time. Walter was then still only a boy, and the monk Adam Elder was appointed his tutor. In 1556 the young abbot was sent by the bishop to Paris in the care of Elder to study Greek, Latin and philosophy.

On 5th December 1553 the bishop of Orkney was papal mandatory to give possession of the abbey of Paisley to the new commendator. He then left for his fifth and last visit to his diocese.

Notes

1. The Hamilton Papers. vol.1 (106) p.132
2. Ibid. (107) p.137
3. Ibid. (108) p.137
4. Ibid. (109) p.141
5. Sir Ralph Sadler "Embassy toScotland 1543". p.167
6. Calderwood: "Historie of the Kirk in Scotland" p.171
7. Sanderson, Margaret H.B. "Cardinal of Scotland" p.179
8. John Knox: "History of the Reformation in Scotland" Bk.i. p.264
9. R.K.Hannay: "The College of Justice" (Stair Soc. 1990) pp.76 ff.108
10. Craven:"History of the Church in Orkney, prior to 1558" p.168
11. Calderwood p. 262.
12. Privy Council Minutes 1553

6 Vespers

Ecce quam bonum et quam jucundum habitare fratres in unum.

i. The last visit to Orkney

Although his stays in Orkney were relatively brief - as far as is known, he never visited Shetland - yet it is clear that he took great pains to see that the affairs of the diocese were conducted in strict accordance with the precepts and customs of the catholic church. He was undoubtedly a stern disciplinarian, but a fair one, and concerned to see that no scandal should attach to the members of the chapter that served the cathedral church of his diocese. At this visit he arranged for the perpetual vicars and choristers to reside in a separate house. For the subdean, who would be in charge of the vicars in the absence of the provost, he had a suitable chamber constructed within the house with an inner closet and cellar. In this way the subdean would be in a better position to look after the "learning, morals and right judgement" of his charges. The chaplains and choristers were obliged to reside in the chambers assigned to them and observe the conditions appointed by the bishop and chapter. The subdean was required to sit at table with the choristers in hall and take note of any that were absent at night and deal with them as he saw fit. This suggests that not everyone had behaved, in the bishop's absence, with the decorum expected of them. Penalties were ascribed for failure to observe the rules.

One of the orders made by the bishop during this visit was for a requiem mass to be celebrated by the vicars and choristers on the anniversary of the archdeacon of Orkney's death and for his predecessor and successors. During the present archdeacon's life five masses for the five wounds of Christ were to be celebrated at St. Andrew's altar once a year.

Once again his visit to Orkney was cut short by a call to return to Edinburgh at a time of crisis.

ii. Curator to the queen

The position of the governor, Arran, who was now also Duke of Chatelherault, had been becoming increasingly precarious especially since the queen, having reached the age of twelve was deemed to be the "perfect age" at which she could choose her own curators. Parliament also considered that she could, if she so wished, dispose of the regency. Moreover, in England, King Edward had died and been succeeded by Mary, the daughter of the catholic Catherine of Aragon, and the threat from a protestant England had, for the time being, been removed. In 1554 Marie of Guise, the queen mother, assured the Scots that, under her guidance, the queen would continue to govern them according to their own laws and that James Hamilton, the duke of Chatelherault, would still be acknowledged heir should the queen bear no children. In April 1554 the regency was transferred to Marie of Guise. Chatellerault and the dowager queen agreed that the lords should appoint curators to the young queen who would authorise and oversee the transfer of power to the dowager. The bishop of Orkney, who was already close to the queen, was chosen as a curator and agreed to serve, at the special request of the dowager and the duke, for this one purpose only, and took the oath to administer the transfer justly. Whereupon, on the bishop's advice and authority, the young queen discharged the governor who renounced all claims. Bishop Robert then ordered the seal to be affixed to the deed which he countersigned and, with the queen dowager, presented it to parliament for ratification. He advised the queen to appoint a commissioner to attend to any supplications from the duke of Chatelherault. Then with the other members of the three estates ordered the documents to be registered and the duke of Chatelherault, as governor, was finally discharged.

By the beginning of 1555 the bishop had paid the full 4000 merks to the queen in respect of the barony of Far (part of the escheated McKay lands) and requested that the ex-governor, the lord high treasurer and the queen's curator agree the warrant for the lands of Far but the lords of council prevaricated. Then the queen's advocate moved a case against the bishop to reduce the infeftment of the lands and again the bishop called upon the Duke of Chatelherault and the treasurer to give warrant for the lands. The lords then decided to seek further legal advice, it being suggested that the gift of Far was of no effect since it had been given during the queen's minority. Reid's advocate protested before the lords, who remained difficult to persuade. It seems likely that the warrant was eventually agreed since the bishop's heirs eventually came into possession of the McKay lands of Strathnaver, McKay having failed to repay the mortgage.

iii. Legal and other matters in the 1550s

The 1550s were busy years for Robert Reid especially in his capacity as President of the College of Justice but he still had time for other interests. Among these he would seem to have developed a taste for the study of natural history. Conrad Gesner, professor of philosophy and natural history at Zurich and a classical scholar, had compiled an Historia Animalium, an account of all known fauna. Gesner's chief interest was in botany although he also wrote on many other subjects including medicine and mineralogy. He had been recommended to approach Reid for some pictures of rare fishes. These the bishop sent him. Gesner then wrote back to the bishop asking him to add names to them. Which fish it was that Reid sent pictures and descriptions of to Gesner is difficult to determine from the vast range of genuine and mythological creatures which were included in Gesner's massive volume on sea creatures. There is one which he calls 'De Hyaena Cetacea' (the Hyena Whale) that is described as having been exhibited by Olaus in Denmark. It was said to resemble a pig, and had appeared in the sea near the island of Thule to the north of the Orcades in the year 1537! He calls it Hyena but admits that the nose is very piglike and the ears not those of a marine animal. Most wonderful are the three eyes that appear on the side of its body! Reid had contact with the Danish king to whom he sent an account of the Orkney islands and may perhaps have obtained a picture of this wonderful creature from him.

Ferrerio, writing to Reid from Paris at this time, asked the bishop to obtain for him a copy of Buchanan's Scottish History and commended to him Edward Henryson, a Greek and Latin scholar who, on Reid's recommendation, became Master of the sang-school in Edinburgh in 1553 and, by 1556, was receiving a yearly pension of £100 for teaching laws and Greek.

Pressure was being brought upon the bishops to pay their contribution toward the College but Reid, as President, protested that most of them had either already paid or were ready to to do so.

Ever more land disputes and claims came Reid's way. He acted as arbitrator in a case between David Bruce of Kinnaird and Edward Bruce of Easter Kennet - the latter of whom had married the bishop's sister, Christian - over the redemption of the lands of Hiltoncroft and Craighill. He was commissioner for letting the lands of the earldom of Marchlands and the lordship of Dundee. Another cause, of long standing, involved the Earl and lady of Crawford who were engaged in a dispute with the master of Crawford that had lasted from 1545 to 1557. The bishop held consultations and meetings with the parties at his house but was unfortunately unable to get them to reach final agreement over the amount to be given for the lands of Carny.

In 1554 the bishop had been chosen by Alexander, Lord Lovat, to act as arbitrator between himself and his mother, Dame Janet Ross, Lady Lovat, who claimed that her son had interfered with her "widow's thirds". The arbitration decreed that Lord Lovat should "stand kindly " to his mother and also pay half the tocher for his sister. As he had failed to do either of these things the case was brought to the supreme court in 1557. The President and lords of council then decreed that Lord Lovat should be distrained to the sum of £4228.16s and ordered not to molest his mother.

Robert Carnegie of Kinnaird appointed the bishop to arbitrate in the event of any dispute between his heirs and executors. Like many others he believed that he could trust Robert Reid to act with scrupulous fairness in such matters and, as in the case against Alexander Lord Lovat, not be swayed by considerations of past or present friendship.

In the reigns of James IV and V acts had been passed regulating the standard weights to be used in buying and selling throughout the burghs and country and abolishing the use of local measures. These acts had not been strictly followed and parliament now passed an act appointing the bishop of Orkney and others to meet in Edinburgh and make them effective. The elwand, quart, pint, firlot, pack, stone and pound were ordered to be brought from Stirling, Linlithgow and Lanark and a universal standard of weights and measures to be established by the beginning of November 1555. The measure of water, it seems, was to be left to local custom. It is doubtful however whether this act was of any more effect than the previous ones!

All medieval ports were subject to outbreaks of plague and other diseases brought in by ships arriving from foreign parts. The Scottish ports were no exception. In 1555 ships arriving with wine from Bordeaux in particular were believed to be infected with the 'pest'. In December the bishop of Orkney, on behalf of the council, ordered the mace-bearers and other officers of arms at Edinburgh, Leith and other east coast ports to proclaim that all masters, skippers, mariners and ship owners should not land any passengers or wares before the provost and bailies of the town had inspected their ships for the presence of any sick person aboard or any danger of sickness. Such quarantine measures would have done much to reduce the incidence of disease, although it would be centuries before ship born plague would be eliminated from western ports.

Reid was still vicar of Kirkcaldy in the the mid 1550s when he received a letter from the curate Matthew Paterson (also known as Litstar) requesting various things for divine worship for "your flock of Kirkcaldy". The curate quotes Deuteronomy (25.4) "one shalt not muzzle the ox when he treadeth out the corn" adding "nor close the viscera of compassion to the servants of the altars...therefore...be generous". It seems possible that the bishop was generous, at least to the extent of providing a new bell, for that in the old church, which was recast twice in the eighteenth century, is inscribed "made 1553".

In September 1557 Robert Reid finally gave up the vicarage of Kirkcaldy being succeeded by Mr.James Moutray. At about the same time he disposed of four crofts that he owned, south of the Burgh of Elgin, to three chaplains of Moray cathedral, William and Douglas Alexander and John Sinclair.

In or about the year 1556 Cardinal Sermonta had suggested to Pope Paul IV that "honest and upright" prelates should be appointed, acceptable to the queen, who would order the correction of nuns, compel abbots to undertake all necessary repairs to their monasteries and prohibit trade on a large scale by prelates who were not hesitating to seek gain by buying villages and estates. It was a very worthy and necessary action. Unfortunately the cardinal was clearly not well informed concerning the Scottish prelacy since, in addition to the bishop of Orkney, who was an excellent choice, he proposed bishop Hepburn of Moray and bishop Chisholm of Dunblane both notorious debauchers! At this time a certain John Row, who made a business of selling of benefices, was, in the course of this business, directing a mass of letters to the bishop of Orkney - at the total cost of twenty-six shillings!

In addition to sending his nephew, Walter Reid the new abbot of Kinloss, to Paris in the care of Adam Elder, the bishop is credited with arranging for a number of other young men to receive their education there.

In 1556 he was tutor to another of his nephews, John Reid of Aikenhead, the son of his brother David. The bishop and his nephew, John, made a contract with James Scott, the son of John Scott of Spencerfield, concerning a decree by the sheriffs of Fife over the lands of Saline Wester and Prinlaws. He took into his own care and tutelage yet another of his nephews, Adam Blackwood, the orphaned son of his sister Helen Reid and William Blackwood. Adam Blackwood enjoyed Reid's love and protection during the bishop's life but the bishop's death deprived him of the means to continue his education in Paris, a few years after entering the university. However James Beaton, bishop of Glasgow, a close friend, obtained him a teaching post at the university on the recommendation of queen Mary (who remembered his uncle, Robert Reid's services). He subsequently became a counsellor of the parliament of Poitiers. Adam's brother, Henry, and four other of Reid's nephews also benefited from a Paris education at the bishop's expense. Although there is no contemporary evidence for these acts of generosity on the bishop's part, which are reported by later chroniclers, they would certainly have been in character. They may also have added strength to the belief that Robert Reid had himself been educated at the university of Paris.

In January 1556 the bishop was mandatory for Pope Paul IV, for entrusting the priory of Inchmahome to David Erskine.

Later that year Reid was in attendance on the queen regent as she progressed through the realm in company with lords and other noblemen and her French counsellors; first to Inverness in July where she held a justice court. In August Bishop Robert was "lord compositor" for remission to John Hay of Park for having intercommunicated with rebels and murderers and for the "destruction of grey deer, forests and for oppressions". At Inverness Robert Reid introduced, Alexander, Lord Lovat (with whom he was still on friendly terms despite the dispute that the young Lord Lovat had had with his mother) to the queen dowager who requested him to act against John Mudertach, an outlaw, with whom Lovat himself had a quarrel. However the bishop dissuaded the queen from pursuing the matter.

The queen mother then moved on to Elgin where bishop Robert's procurator presented Thomas Tulloch to her justiciary court for the lands of Kinloss, and the bishop leased the lands of Dullater to James Ogilvy of Findlater.

The queen then moved on to Banff and Aberdeen where the bishop, in company with others, had a diplomatic function to perform. Here, in

October 1556, a peace treaty was concluded with the countess of East Friesland. The treaty of 1547 with Friesland was due to expire and Ann, countess of East Friesland, sent her ambassador, Hoitet Tjaberberen to renew it for one hundred years. The envoy met with George, earl of Huntley, the chancellor, the bishop of Orkney, John Bellenden of Auchnoul, justice clerk, and Robert Carnegie of Kinnaird. The new treaty was signed, hostilities were to be abolished and freedom of trade assured.

The following winter the queen regent sent the Earl of Huntly to "bring the highlanders to their duty". With the counsel and advice of the bishop of Orkney who, as commendator of Beauly, had had some contact with the highlands, and other counsellors, a more suitable manner of holding courts at Inverness, Elgin and Forres was devised, for hearing the libels and accusations of the highlanders.

iv. A French alliance and an English peace

In 1556 the regent, Marie of Guise, was anxious to have the Scots invade England. However the lords, despite a victory over English troops at Tweedsdale, were reluctant to pursue the war after three months and told the regent that they would maintain the border, a job which they left largely to French troops, but not proceed further south. The army was then disbanded. The regent decided that the only way in which she might prevail over the lords was to get the young queen married to the dauphin as soon as possible. She hoped that as a result the influence of the Scottish lords would be diminished by the presence of the queen's husband. She therefore sent letters to France to hasten the marriage.

The king of France, who was beset by his own problems with fighting the Spanish, had, up till then, not greatly favoured the marriage. He now came to the conclusion that the alliance with the Scots might enable him to avail himself of Scottish forces against the English. Henry II of France therefore wrote to the estates of Scotland reminding them of the proposal originally made in 1545 for the alliance of the queen and the dauphin and suggesting that the engagement be solemnized on 6th January 1558. The letter received in October 1557 "...well interspersed with marks of love and good-will drew the minds of all to the attachment to princes". The regent summoned parliament where the letter was read and the three estates appointed the following commissioners to treat for the marriage with the king of France and the dauphin - James, archbishop of Glasgow; David, bishop of Ross; Robert, bishop of Orkney; earl George of Rothes;

earl Gilbert of Cassillis; Lord James Stewart, prior of St. Andrew's; lord James Fleming; lord George Seton and John Erskine of Dun, provost of Montrose, to represent the burghs. The regent was to be represented by her mother, Antoinette de Bourbon, dowager duchess of Guise.

Taxation of £15000 was to be raised for the ambassadors' expenses. The regent and the estates guaranteed to pay ransom for any commissioner taken prisoner and, should any commissioner be slain or die whilst on service, their heirs to have ward and marriage free; the wives and children to have tacks of the commissioner's lands for five years and, if the widow remarried, the son or eldest daughter to have them; the nearest kin of a prelate to have his benefice. All judicial processes, if any, against any commissioner to cease. The duke of Chatelherault hastened to seek assurance that his right to succeed should be upheld in the event of the queen's failure to produce an heir.

Now the queen dowager was ready to make peace with England. Once again Robert Reid was required to act as one of the Scottish commissioners to treat with the English and seek redress of the wrongs on the borders. This time the discussions would take place with the representatives of an English queen, Mary Tudor.

On the 11th June 1557 the commissioners met the English at Carlisle. They then separated to talk to their opposite numbers and the bishop of Orkney held discussions with the bishop of Durham. He called for equal restitution on both sides in order to preserve a friendly atmosphere regardless of the wishes of the French. The following morning bishop Robert asked for a meeting with another of the English commissioners and repeated what he claimed he had always maintained, that he loved and honoured the queen of England above all princesses in the world next to his own mistress and that he never prayed for his own mother but that he also prayed for queen Mary. He trusted that the peace would never be broken in her days. "God forfend that plague", he is said to have exclaimed, "for if the two great and mighty princesses took this different, there is no likelihood of peace or end of war in Christendom". When it was remarked that the queen of England showed a desire for peace having sent ambassadors to Calais for peace between France and the Emperor, the bishop of Orkney remarked: "It is true but yet I do not despair and all shall be well if the queen of Scotland might speak to the French king either at Michaelmas or Candlemas next, as she intended, and see the queen of England on her way; if this could be achieved it might be a great means of making the entire Christendom quiet." When it was remarked that the queen of Scotland might be involved in an invasion of England as a consequence of the rupture between England and France the bishop assured the commissioners "upon my soul" that no such thing was intended and he gave them two or three examples of Scotland's having remained true to England when there had previously been war between England and France.

In order to ensure peace on the borders the bishop suggested that, on the departure of the commissioners, wardens should be charged with maintaining that peace, on pain of death, at least for the next month or two until the princesses' pleasure should be known. The other commissioners agreed and accordingly issued orders to that effect.

The somewhat fulsome language employed by Reid was, of course, the language of diplomacy and he was nothing if not a consummate diplomat. However he no doubt expressed such feelings with greater sincerity than he would have done had it been Henry VIII with whom he was dealing. Mary was, after all, the daughter of Katherine and a staunch catholic who burnt more heretics than had cardinal Beaton! Whether or not the bishop altogether approved this, he would have been happy to have seen catholicism restored in England.

There was much coming and going between the commissioners and the regent and lords, who remained at Newbattle. On the English side Dr. Martyn conferred with his council and returned to assure Reid that the peace would be kept unless broken by the Scots, whom he feared might attack England if the English invaded France. Reid assured him that Scotland had no intention of making war against England and that the commission would proclaim peace for the next month or two pending the final decision of the sovereigns. Agreements were reached on the exchange of prisoners and to secure settlement on the borders, and peace was proclaimed at the High Cross at Carlisle with a meeting arranged to take place at Riddingburn on 15th September for final agreement. The Scots commissioners then returned to Scotland and met the regent and lords who had remained at Newbattle. There the regent appointed the earl of Huntly to be general lieutenant on the borders.

Huntly remained at Duns and, despite all that had been agreed by the commissioners, made preparations for war and ordered raids on England. Two foraging expeditions being mounted at the towns of Coquetdale and Cornhill. In addition two of the late king's bastard sons raised a force to burn villages on the borders and drive off cattle causing panic among the citizens of Berwick. The council of England, understandably, considered that this came too soon after all the solemn proclamations of amity and sent Lord Wharton to find out whether the regent of Scotland really wanted war or peace.

Just to remind the Scots what war might mean, the English issued a proclamation licensing all English subjects to act against French and Scottish ships and to stop all communications between Scotland and Berwick. The queen of England then persuaded her husband, Philip of Spain, to send ships to stop trade between Scotland and Flanders and to attack the Scots should they fail to keep the peace. She also sent Sir John Clare to harass the west coast of Scotland and to burn Kirkwall, possibly to remind the bishop of his fair words at Carlisle (and not in retribution for the bishop's part in arranging the Scottish queens marriage to the dauphin, as has been suggested, since he had not then been appointed a commissioner for the marriage).

A considerable force landed at Kirkwall with eight to ten pieces of artillery. However the islanders were not so easily cowed and attacked the English landing party killing some three hundred of them and driving the rest back into the sea. A typical Orkney storm then blew up forcing the ships out to sea and preventing many from reaching them, so that two hundred men were said to have been drowned. It was reported that three captains were among those who lost their lives, incuding the admiral - however the latter was later seen to be alive in September of 1557. The English artillery and baggage as well as quantities of gold and silver remained ashore and the prisoners taken paid large sums in ransom, so that the outcome proved extremely profitable to the Orcadians!

At the end of 1557 another job fell to the lot of the Robert Reid. An oversman was required to be chosen by the members of the assize to perambulate the lands of Invernety, belonging to the earl of Marischal, and of Gask, belonging to the master of Errol. In the event of their failing to make the appointment, the bishop of Orkney was required to undertake the task.

And in January 1558 the bishop had his procurator raise objections. on behalf of Margaret and Katherine Dumbreck - the latter being the wife of Reid's nephew John, to both of whom the bishop had been tutor - to the actions of Marjorie Forbes, Lady Tercer, over the lands of Miltown and Dumbreck,

In the same month, Adam Elder reported to the bishop on the progress that his nephew, the new abbot of Kinloss, had been making in his studies. Also at this time Elder dedicated a collection of his sermons to the bishop in reverence and gratitude, "to whom, after God, he owed everything".

v. Last will and testament

At the end of January 1558 Robert Reid attended the last session of the College of Justice of which he had been a member for twenty-five years and over which he had presided for the past eight. He is said to have bid them farewell yet he could scarcely have known that it would be his last session. Maybe, however, he had some foreboding for, before his departure for France, he made his will. The actual document has not survived but its contents can be arrived at, at least in part, from consideration of other documents. The essential bequests were:

1. A legacy of 800 merks to the children of mr. Edward Bruce of Kennet, who was married to his sister, Christian.

2. One thousand merks to add to the dowry for his niece, Catherine Reid.

3. Four hundred marks each to his nephew James and niece Margaret. (Their brother John Reid of Aikenhead would receive the bishop's lands of Blair of Forth, Strentoun, Collistoun, and Schramylhill either by testament or as heir to the estates).

4. The 4000 merks which he had in wadset of the lands of Strathnaver, when it should be recovered, plus another 4000 merks "from his awin proper guidis and geir", 8000 merks in all, to be used for the purchase of the tenement with a yard and pertinents of the late Sir John Ramsay of Balmane on the south side of Edinburgh, on which a college should be built containing three schools:

one for bairns to be taught grammar; a second for them to be taught poetry and oratory, together with a chamber for the regents, and a third for teaching civil and canon law. The foundation of this college to be undertaken with the counsel of three procurators, James Macgill of Nether Rankeilour, clerk register and Senator of the College of Justice; Mr. Thomas Maccalzean of Cliftonhall, an advocate and later provost of Edinburgh and Mr. Abraham Creichton, provost of the collegiate church of Dunglas, Senator of the college of Justice and official of Lothian, who will pursue the payment of the 4000 merks owing on the lands of Strathnaver.

It is claimed by many authorities today that Reid left 8,000 merks for the foundation of a University in Edinburgh. Grant in Cassel's 'Old and New Edinburgh' writes: "Of the four Scottish Universities, the youngest is Edinburgh, a perfectly Protestant foundation, as the other three were established under the catholic regime; yet the merit of originating the idea of academical institutions for the metropolis is due to Robert Reid, who, in 1558, six years before the date of Queen Mary's charter, 'had bequeathed to the town of Edinburgh the sum of 8,000 merks for the purpose of erecting a University in the city.'"[1]

It will be remembered however that in the terms of the will no mention was made of a university.

The Library of the University was begun with the donation of his collection of books by Clement Little, at the suggestion of his brother William Little, who almost certainly knew Reid as he came to own Reid's copy of Johannes Herold's 'Orthodoxographid' and, in 1561 acted as curator for John Reid of Aikenhead, Robert Reid's nephew and pupil, "in the absence of Walter Reid, abbot of Kinloss, now being in France". In addition Clement Little was one of the judges of the Commissary Court in June 1564 when John and Walter compeared as executors and "allegit that the saud umquhil bischop befoir his deceis maid his testament and nominated thame his executouris testamentaris thairin…". James Kirk suggests in his introduction to "Edinburgh University Library 1580-1988" [2] that this lends support to the idea that Reid might have had the founding of the University in mind.

However what Reid, in fact, intended was a far more modest establishment. Unfortunately, as Nowosilski shows [3], sufficient moneys were never available to establish the schools that he planned and certainly nowhere near enough to fund a university. It has been suggested that he also left moneys for the maintenance of poor gentlemen's sons at the universities of Aberdeen, St. Andrews and Glasgow but this may simply have been based on Adam Elder's words: "it is not necessary to relate any other charitable works in which his beneficence is engaged as… giving in marriage girls whose possessions are too scanty to enable them to pay their dowry, as liberal support of many promising youths of noble birth in studying letters." Elder was, in all probability referring to the times when, during his life, the bishop had come to the aid of these girls and boys.

As executors of his will, Reid named his nephew, John Reid of Aikenhead; his nephew, Walter Reid, abbot of Kinloss; Sir Robert Carnegie of Kinnaird, knight; Thomas Tulloch of Fluris, constable of Orkney and chamberlain to the bishop; William Forsyth, subprior of Kinloss and the bishop's attendant and schir John Anderson, a canon of the cathedral in Kirkwall.

The will was signed in Edinburgh on 6th February 1558.

vi. Voyage to France

On the very day that the will was signed Robert Reid and the other commissioners, joined by the lord Lyon King at Arms and Ross herald, set sail for France from Kirkcaldy. The escorting vessels left from Leith to join them. At the last moment a large number of writs arrived in haste from the queen regent. The convoy was given the signal to start by the firing of a gun.

Reid travelled in company with the earl of Rothes, a number of other gentlemen and their servants, in one of the boats; their horses being carried in another alongside. Among Reid's companions was the archdeacon of Shetland, Jerome Cheyne, a 'valued servant' of the bishop, according to Donaldson[4]. He had been a notary and one time accused, with his brother, James, of assaulting two other men in 1547; he was parson of Torry and had been presented with the archdeaconry in 1554.

Reid's very last sight of Scotland was the one place in which he had long held a parochial benefice, Kirkcaldy.

The voyage was a stormy one from the start, with thunder and lightening and gale force winds. Abreast of St. Abb's Head the boat carrying the horses sank. Among those who perished was the son of the captain of Reid's boat and it fell to the bishop to give him what comfort he could.

That was not the end of the disasters on the voyage for, as they neared the coast of France, Captain Watterton's ship carrying many gentlemen and a great number of valuables ("furniture for the marriage") foundered.

The ship carrying Reid and the earl of Rothes was also in trouble and began to sink. William Gibson, the skipper of one of the escorting vessels from Leith, abandoned his own ship in an attempt to rescue the bishop and the earl. His attempt ended in disaster. Failing to reach them and, unable to return to his own ship, his small boat capsized and he was drowned. When they must almost have abandoned all hope of rescue a fishing boat appeared and the earl of Rothes made a successful attempt to get clear of the sinking ship. The crew of the fishing boat took the earl on board and then rescued the bishop and as many others as the boat could hold without capsizing. They were landed on shore on the sands near Boulogne. There, with nothing but what they stood up in and some documents they had managed to salvage, they watched helplessly as those other gentlemen of their party, left aboard the ship, and who could not be safely accommodated in the little fishing boat, perished. Much in the way of silver, jewels and clothes also went down with the ships.

Disasters at sea were all too frequent when ships were so much at the mercy of the elements but this voyage would appear to have had more than its fair share of them.

If it should be thought that the bishop, at least, as a man of God, might have given up his place in the boat to others, it should be remembered that he was on a commission for his queen and this would have had priority over any thoughts of saving himself or others. Moreover the only things the earl and bishop made sure of saving from the wreck were the writs entrusted to them.

Meanwhile the remaining commissioners had managed to land safely at Dieppe after a voyage lasting five days. They waited for two or three days for the others to arrive. When they failed to turn up, they assumed that all aboard the sunken ships had been lost. They waited no longer but hastened on to Paris where they arrived on 20th February 1558.

The earl and the bishop meanwhile managed to acquire horses in the neighbourhood and rode to join them. It has been said that they rode from Calais to Le Havre by which route they would have passed Dieppe. If so they presumably found that the others, believing them to be drowned, had already left that town and set off for Paris.

The bishop and earl arrived safely at their destination without further mishap and there joined their fellow commissioners to represent the estates of Scotland. Together once more, the Scots set out to meet the king of France and the dauphin in order to fulfill their commission. They had been instructed make sure that all the conditions, laid down by the estates of Scotland for the wedding of their queen to the Dauphin, were understood and accepted by the French.

vii. A secret agreement and a public one

The court was not in Paris when the commissioners arrived there so that, the following month, they left to go to Moret. Here they were met by the Venetian ambassador and the papal legate. From Moret they travelled nine kilometres to Fontainebleau. Here, at last, they were received by the king, the cardinal and the French nobility with great honour.

Queen Mary, now that both she and the dauphin were of age, appointed her grandmother together with the commissioners sent by the estates, to be her commissioners for treating with the king of France. Owing to the delay caused by the various mishaps on the voyage the wedding was postponed until eight days after Easter.

The formality of examining the parties for any impediment due to consanguinity was undertaken by Laurence Lenzi, bishop of Fermo and nuncio in France and Nicholas de Pelleve, bishop of Amiens, on the orders of Cardinal Antonino Trivulzio, papal *legate de latere* in France. Cardinal Trivulzio then dispensed the dauphin and queen Mary of the impediment that a fourth degree of consanguinity would have imposed. At the request of the king of France the calling of banns was dispensed with and the king agreed to Mary's request for the duke of Guise to be her curator in France.

At the beginning of April, before the wedding, the French king, Henry II, persuaded the young queen to sign three documents which would not have had the approval of the Scottish delegation had they been made aware of them. The documents agreed the following:

1. Considering the great expenditure laid out by the king of France for the defence of Scotland against the English and that the preservation of Scotland from the danger of total ruin was due entirely to France, the king of France, in the case of queen Mary's death without issue, is to have all the revenue and full possession of her realm until the sum of 1,000,000 of gold for that defence had been reimbursed.

2. Considering the protection of Scotland and goodness of Henry who maintained her at his cost, she makes a pure and free gift of Scotland to the king of France in case of her death except the rights that England may have.

3. Having been informed of the instructions which the commissioners of Scotland had, that in secret scheming there is desire to assign her realm, in case of her death without issue, to a native nobleman and considering that she cannot oppose it openly because of fear, she protests that, whatever consent she has given or might give to the articles sent by the estates of Scotland for the event of her death without issue, she would do it against her will and the disposition, made by her in favour of France, remain.

Having obtained the queen's signature to these documents in secret, the king of France and the dauphin nevertheless ratified the act of the Scottish parliament concerning the marriage. This agreed that the queen's next of kin would succeed to the Scottish crown and that it would be the obligation of the French to help the duke of Chatellerault to succeed to the throne in the event of the queen dying without heirs. Queen Mary, on her part, ratified Henry II's obligation of 1549 to obtain the discharge of the duke from the administration during her minority and a promise to observe the privileges of Scotland.

By the terms of the settlement, agreed by the Scots, the queen was to receive a dowry of £60,000 tournois to be secured on the duchy, county and lands of Touraine and Poitou, should the dauphin predecease her after he had succeeded to the crown. If he predeceased her whilst still dauphin, she would receive a pension of £30,000 yearly. If the queen survived her husband she might either remain in France or return to Scotland with her servants, remarry and take those things usually possessed by the queens of France after the decease of their kings. These rights she would enjoy whether or not she were to have a family. Her eldest son to succeed to the throne of Scotland and to take the coats of arms of the two kingdoms united. If the eldest daughter succeeds to the throne and marries with the consent of the king of France, she will receive a dowry of 400,000 crowns and the remaining daughters 300,000 crowns each.

Immediately after the marriage the commissioners would be expected to take an oath of fidelity to the dauphin in the name of the estates of Scotland for as long as he is married. The dauphin to have the title of King of Scotland (his arms quartered with those of Scotland) and on succeeding to the throne of France to have the coats of arms of the two kingdoms united under the same crown. The contract was signed at the Louvre on 19th April 1558. It seems clear that the Scottish commissioners had had no knowledge of the secret agreement between the queen and the French at this time.

viii. The betrothal

The marriage ceremonies of royalty in the sixteenth century were conducted with displays of great extravagance, in order to outshine those of rival monarchs. Pageants would be staged, often under the direction of one of the leading artists of the period. The wedding of a queen of Scotland to a future king of France therefore required the most elaborate preparation. The tailors were kept busy embroidering clothes to enhance the magnificence of the participants; stages were erected within the reception hall of the new palace of the Louvre; a wooden bridge with a gallery was constructed from the courtyard of the bishop's house across the square before the church to the portal of Notre Dame.

Within the palace cardinal Trivulzio once again dispensed any impediments of consanguinity and the engagement of Mary and the dauphin was formally performed "per verba de Praesenti", the vows being given in the presence of the king and queen of France and of many cardinals and nobility. No doubt Robert Reid was present and with a much higher profile than had been accorded him at the wedding of James V to princess Madeleine.

The contract of marriage was signed by King Henry, queen Catherine and the dauphin on the French side and by queen Mary, Antoinette, her grandmother, and the Scottish commissioners, on the Scottish side, in the presence of all the great noblemen and clerics assembled. The wedding was arranged to take place on the following Sunday. A dance followed the betrothal ceremony at which the young Scottish queen partnered the French king.

On the same day King Henry and the dauphin ratified the Scottish act acknowledging that in the event of the queen's death her next of kin would succeed her and that, should she die childless, Chatelherault would be next in line to the Scottish throne. The dowry and other financial matters were already settled by the marriage contract.

After the betrothal ceremony the master of ceremonies, on behalf of the king, invited the provost, merchants and aldermen of the city to attend the marriage on Sunday - and afterwards to supper!

ix. The royal wedding

Chroniclers (as described by Nowosilski[5]) have recorded the ceremonies and entertainments that took place on Sunday 22nd April 1558. Although they may not themselves have been present and had to rely on the accounts of eye witnesses, it can be assumed that their descriptions were, on the whole, reasonably accurate. They certainly convey a flavour of the occasion. [Such extravagant ceremonies can no longer be seen at royal or any other weddings and the closest we come at the present day to such scenes as were witnessed in Paris in 1558 would be at the opening and closing ceremonies of the Olympic Games!]

On the day of the wedding, before the great doorway of the church, royal cloth was spread, strewn with fleur-de-lys. The same cloth was also laid within the church together with tapestries bearing the coats-of-arms of the king and of Scotland.

The provost and city councillors, having assembled at the door of the town hall at 7.00 a.m, were joined by companies of archers, cross-bowmen and harquebusiers of the city and ten sergeants with silver boats on their shoulders. The councillors mounted mules and the whole procession made its way at 9.00 a.m. to Notre Dame. They entered by way of the wooden bridge, which had been covered with ivy, and took their place in the choir. Here they found the accountants and officers of justice already installed. They soon had to make room for the mint masters on their arrival. Opposite them were the members of the court of parliament in scarlet robes of velvet with furred hoods on their shoulders, their president wearing a biretta. After 10 a.m. the French and Scottish lords arrived, together with the university staff and the clergy, the ambassadors, the cardinal Chatilton and many other high ranking Frenchmen.

Meanwhile, in the bishop's house, the royal family were being entertained by the Swiss, in livery, playing tambourines, trumpets and fifes. Later the Swiss left the bishop' house and crossed the bridge to the cathedral where they played until 11 a.m. Many noblemen standing on this bridge and obstructing the view of the people were made to move by the duke of Guise.

Eustache du Bellay, the bishop of Paris, with the cross and two acolytes carrying silver candlesticks went to the portal to meet the nuptial procession. First came the players in red and yellow livery playing canticles and motets praising God, on trumpets, clarions. hautboys, flageolets, viols, violins, citherns and guitars. They were followed by one hundred gentlemen of the royal household, princes, abbots, eighteen bishops - including Robert, bishop of Orkney - many archbishops and the cardinals of Bourbon, Lorraine, Guise, Sens, Meudon and Lenoncourt and Cardinal Trivulzio, the papal legate, preceded by a golden cross and mace. Next came the dauphin led by the king of Navarre and the dukes of Orleans and Angouleme. Following the Dauphin came the queen of Scotland led by the king of France with his right hand and the duke of Lorraine with his left. The queen was dressed in a lily-like gown of white velour covered with precious stones and white embroidery with two ladies carrying her very long train. Round her neck she wore a jewelled collar and on her head a crown of gold enriched with pearls, diamonds, rubies, sapphires and emeralds and hanging from it a carbuncle worth 500,000 crowns. The bride was followed by the queen of France with the prince of Conde; the queen of Navarre, the king's sister; Marguerite duchess of Berry and many other princesses and ladies.

The bishop of Orkney and the other Scottish bishops had been given golden copes and golden mitres adorned with precious stones and the

Scottish earls and lords the regalia of the order of St. Michael in addition to many other valuable presents.

At the door of the cathedral a stage had been erected and here the king removed a ring from his finger and handed it to the cardinal of Bourbon, archbishop of Rouen, who married the Scottish queen and the dauphin. The bishop of Paris then delivered the sermon.

Once again the duke of Guise accompanied by two heralds had to clear the noblemen away from the bridge to give the people of Paris, in the street and at their windows, a better view of the proceedings. Then the heralds shouted "Largesse" and threw gold and silver coins to the multitude. This caused considerable chaos among the crowd as they fought for the money; some of them fainted, others had their clothes torn from their backs, gentlemen their cloaks, gentlewomen their farthingales, merchants their gowns, masters of arts their hoods, students their cornet caps, religious men their scapulas. One young barefoot Franciscan friar managed to get four times as much as his companions. Asked why he kept the money contrary to his vows he answered "If St. Francis himself were present here he would put to his hand as I have done to the laud of God and the honour of the marriage".

Meanwhile the procession entered the church with the cardinal of Bourbon, the bishop of Paris and the other bishops leading the way to the choir which was spread with a carpet of golden cloth. The king was seated on the right with the queen behind him and opposite them the dauphin and the new dauphiness. The bishop of Paris then celebrated mass during which more gold and silver coins were thrown in the church. After mass the procession returned the way it had come. The king, realising that the people had not had a good view, made the company walk to the edge of the stage to show themselves before returning to the bishop's house. The city men went off to dine opposite Notre Dame before going to a M. Marcel's house to await the call to the royal supper. The contract of marriage and now the wedding itself entitled the dauphin to call himself the dauphin-king and the queen of Scotland became the dauphiness-queen.

During the dinner that followed the wedding the duke of Guise, with the help of the prince of Conde and M. d'Aiz, first gentleman of the royal chamber, gave the instructions. The king ordered the knights of the chamber, messieurs de S. Sever and S.Crespin, to hold up the royal crown of the dauphiness. A ball followed the dinner at which the king danced with the queen of Scotland; the dauphin with his mother; the king of Navarre with Elizabeth, the king's eldest daughter; the duke of Lorraine with his other daughter, Claude; the prince of Conde with the king's sister, Marguerite; the duke of Nevers with the queen of Navarre and the duke of Nemours with the duchess of Guise. They and all the company, with their magnificent dresses, drew the remark "estisne mortales vel non". The ball ended at about four or five in the afternoon.

The whole company then repaired to the palace by way of rue S. Christophe, the bridge Notre Dame and the "pont au change". The kings, princes and lords rode on horses covered with gold and silver cloth; the queens and princesses went in litters and open coaches similarly adorned. The queens of France and Scotland were carried together in a litter with the cardinals of Bourbon and Lorraine riding on either side. There followed the dauphin and the duke of Lorraine, princes, princesses and ladies on horses caparisoned in crimson velvet and golden ornaments. The crowds following were so great that many of the gentlemen could hardly make their way through. At the palace the king received the queen of Scotland; the king of Navarre, the dauphin and the prince of Conde, the queen of France. All then entered the palace.

The city men walked to the palace led by the provost riding on a mule, after the royal party had arrived. Presidents, councillors and officers of the court of parliament in long red robes were also present at the banquet.

At a marble table sat the king and queen of France with the queen of Scotland on their right and the dauphin on their left. The earl of Cassilis was carver to the queen of Scotland and the earl of Rothes her cup-bearer. When royalty were seated players marched in playing on trumpets, clarions, tambourines and other instruments, ahead of one hundred gentlemen carrying maces. These were followed by the stewards of the king, queen, dauphin and dauphiness, twelve in all. Next came the duke of Guise in a golden robe embellished with jewels, he was acting as high steward in the absence of the constable. He introduced each course accompanied by heralds of France and Scotland. After the second course the dauphin presented the heralds with a large silver-gilt jug worth 400 crowns from an array of gold vases and plates on a magnificent sideboard. The heralds then went to shout "largesse" throughout the hall.

At the end of the meal grace was said and the tables removed for the dancing to begin. The queen of Scotland had to have a gentleman hold her train, which was six fathoms long, whilst she danced with Elizabeth, the king's daughter! After her the queen of France and all the rest of the royalty and nobility joined the dancing, the ladies in their riches of gold and silk.

The dancing was followed by masquerade, mummery, ballads and games and exploits of bravery - although there was no tournament or jousting. From the 'golden chamber' there emerged seven planets, dressed as poets, singing songs for the occasion (Mercury with two wings, white satin robe, golden belt and carrying his rod; Mars, armed and Venus dressed as a goddess). After them came horses made of withies covered with gold and silver cloth and led by footmen and made to walk as if they were real. On these rode the dukes of Orleans and Angouleme and the grandchildren of the dukes of Guise and Aumale, in golden and silver clothes. The horses pulled a triumphal chariot by silver cords and in it were seated brightly dressed travellers playing musical instruments and singing hymns and canticles in honour of matrimony. After these came two unicorns (one wonders where they found them!) ridden by young princes arrayed in gold and silver. Next came two white horses pulling an old fashioned type of car in which the nine muses were represented by beautiful girls in green satin, white velours, crimson, blue-grey, and gold and silver clothes, all singing in harmony. More beautifully caparisoned horses followed and many other mummeries, for a further two hours. Then the dancing began again for a half hour.

The pageant returned with six boats entering covered with gold cloth and crimson velvet. Their sails of silver cloth seemed to catch the wind so that they turned this way and that as though floating on water, carried by the waves and propelled by the wind. In each boat was seated a masked prince on one seat with a second seat vacant. After 'sailing' round the hall among the guests they came to the marble table and each prince took a lady from the table to occupy the vacant seat. The duke of Lorraine took Claude, the king's second daughter; the king of Navarre, his queen; the duke of Nemours, Marguerite the king's sister; the prince of Conde, the duchess of Guise; the king took the bride; the dauphin, the queen, his mother. After again circumnavigating the hall the boats took their occupants away to their nights rest![6]

The bride and groom were put to their bed where the marriage was consummated. Both were fifteen years of age.

Thus ended Scotland's day in Paris.

Notes

1. Grant: "History of the University of Edinburgh" in Cassel's "*Old and New Edinburgh*".

2. James Kirk: Intrduction to "*Edinburgh University Library 1580-1988*"

3. Nowosiski p.545 ff.

4. Donaldson '*Reformed by Bishops*" p.29

5. Nowosilski p.345 ff.

6. The charade of gods and goddesses may well have had greater significance than just fanciful entertainment. The medieval interest in astrology among both church and rulers survived, and even experienced a revival, in the Renaissance. Jean Seznec in "The Survival of The Pagan Gods" describes how monarchs - Henry II of France and his queen, Catherine de Medici, being conspicuous among them - took a great interest in astrology and courted the idea of descent from the gods and heroes of the past, such as the Jupiter and Venus, in order to bolster their divine right to rule.

   It will be recalled that Ferrerio rebuked the Franciscans and King James for their credulity at unusual 'signs in the sky'. An admirer of Pico della Mirandola, Ferrerio (and no doubt Reid also) had, like Pico, no time for the current obsession with astrology.

7 Compline

Noctem quietem, et finem perfectum concedat nobis Dominus omnipotens.

i. An unreasonable request

What the bishop thought about all these extravagant festivities which he had, presumably, been obliged to attend, is not recorded. He undoubtedly enjoyed elaborate ceremonial in the service of God, for this would be justified as offering to the Creator all that was best and most beautiful in presentation of the liturgy. Clearly, though, the wedding had been elaborately staged more for the benefit of the participants than for the greater glory of God. The succeeding festivities were entirely for the indulgence of men and women. Nevertheless he would have been less than human not to have taken pleasure in being part of such an occasion, especially as it was in honour of his pupil and ward, the queen of Scotland. At the same time he may well have felt that such extravagant expenditure would have been better put to such causes as education that he held so dear. "Largesse" was all very well but it was but a sop to the few and rarely of benefit to those most in need. However the bishop and his fellow commissioners were soon to be brought down to earth and required to deal with a situation they had not altogether foreseen.

At the conclusion of the marriage ceremonies and festivities the court of France called the Scottish commissioners to appear before the council. There the chancellor asked them to procure the crown and other insignia of the honours of Scotland in order to crown the dauphin, king. The commissioners told the council that they had no commission in that respect. The chancellor hastened to assure them that they would not demand anything that was not within the present power of the commissioners to deliver. However he asked that, when the matter was discussed in the Scottish parliament the commissioners would support the councils request and, with their goodwill, enter an obligation so to do. The commissioners considered such a demand exceedingly shameless and replied that their mission was limited and that it was not in their power to promise anything that was not in their commission. Even if they had unlimited power they could not be expected to require of parliament anything that might bring on them the infamy of traitors, especially as the contents of their commission was known to the council. The Scottish crown, they argued, was imperial, never subject to any other realm nor held by other king and therefore they could not part with it. However if an heir to the dauphin and their queen came to Scotland he would receive the crown with all honours. They would gratify the French in any way that was honourable and asked that the French keep their demands within modest limits. This reply did not please the council so they decided to send a letters to the regent and the Scottish council, reiterating their demands.

The king of France also wrote to the regent, saying that the commissioners had done their duty honourably and praising the devotion of the commissioners to his person, assuring her that it was his desire to keep all the prerogatives intact and even to augment them.

Meanwhile two of the commissioners, who possibly were more amenable to the wishes of the French, were dispatched with the letters to Edinburgh whilst the other lords were held in France for the time being in order to prevent their interfering with the French king's requests.

The queen sent her mother a similar letter.

In order that the Scots might continue to visit their king and queen and to consider the two realms as one, Henry granted them the right to live in France. They might also hold benefices in the country and receive the fruits of those benefices and to acquire and dispose of land to which their heirs might succeed as natives of France. Letters patent to this effect were registered.

Thus whilst appearing to treat the Scots with generosity, the French king was determined, if possible, to get his way and have the dauphin assume the Scottish crown and the French to acquire the 'honours of Scotland'. Everything, in fact, was done to persuade the Scots of the advisability of acceding to the king's demands.

Eventually, after the king believed sufficient time had elapsed for his letter to have reached the regent, the remaining commissioners, who included the bishop of Orkney, were permitted to depart. They took leave of the king at the beginning of August, each of them having been richly rewarded with cups of silver and gold. Queen Mary accompanied them some of the way in gratitude for their part in her nuptials and to show how well they had been received in France.

Toward the end of August they arrived in Dieppe.

Here they embarked for the return to Scotland. The storms that had accompanied their voyage to France returned and their ships were driven back by strong winds into the port of Dieppe. All aboard were suffering from sickness and five of the commission were seriously ill, as was Sir James Colville, laird of Wemyss, and several of their servants.

Within months of their being forced back to France four of the commissioners and Sir James Colville were dead.

Among them was Robert Reid, Bishop of Orkney.

ii. The death of Robert Reid

The dates on which the five men died have been the subject of dispute. However it can be said with a fair degree of accuracy that Robert Reid, the bishop of Orkney, died on the 6th September; the earl of Rothes (who had been tried and acquitted for complicity in the murder of Cardinal Beaton), probably on the 9th of November; the earl of Cassilliss, the High Treasurer, on the 14th November. James, Lord Fleming, hereditary Great Chamberlain of Scotland, who made his testament on the 8th November 1558 and may have returned to Paris before his death, did not die until the early months of 1559. Thomas Tulloch, who had been chamber-child and pursemaster to the bishop for five years and constable of Orkney for ten years and had known the bishop well, gave his death as the 15th September. There must, however, have been considerable delay before he would have received news of the bishop's death. Queen Mary wrote to her mother from the court at Villiers-Cotteret concerning Reid's death on the 16th September. If Tulloch were correct the news would have reached her within a mere twenty-four hours, which is scarcely credible. She sent the letter with Lord Erskine writing: "God willed that the Lord Orkney should be dead, he made the ambassadors send Erskine to me to invite me concerning that which you had granted them, namely that the abbeys of those who died when travelling would be relinquished in favour of their relatives or friends." Robert Reid must have been aware that he was dying when he sent Erskine with the messsage to the queen. Perhaps he wished to ensure that his nephew Walter would receive the priory of Beauly in addition to the abbey of Kinloss in the event of the bishop's death. Reid may even has wished Walter to succeed him as bishop of Orkney.

A popular held belief has been that the commissioners were poisoned, a not altogether uncommon fate, in those times, among princes and politicians who fell foul of the great and powerful. However it would appear at first sight extremely unlikely from the above dates that all four men succumbed to the same poison. It has been pointed out that, for Reid, or any of them, to have travelled some way to Scotland before being forced to return to France, any poison administered must have been abnormally slow acting. However, had a servant been bribed to administer a cumulative poison such as arsenic, or a slow acting one such as Stibnite (Antimony sulphide) or the fungal poison Corticarius orellanus, it is possible to speculate that the older man, bishop Reid, sucumbed more rapidly to its effects whilst Rothes and Cassilliss (and possibly Sir John Colville) were more resistant. Lord Fleming, who may have returned to Paris, could perhaps have received poison at a later date.

Why should anyone choose to poison these commissioners? It has to remembered that two of the commissioners, who were believed to be more sympathetic to the king of France's plan to have the Dauphin crowned and receive the Honours of Scotland, had been sent ahead to plead his cause to the Estates whilst the rest were detained in France. Poisoning may have been a last desperate recourse to prevent the four commissioners thwarting the king's plans. Moreover the king's consort, Catherine de Medici, was, rightly or wrongly, notorious for her use of poison to overcome any opposition to her ambitions. Arsenic and Corticarius being among the poisons she is said to have favoured.

If the idea of poisoning seems far fetched in such circumstances one only has to consider some of the reputed actions of the KGB and the CIA in our present century to realise that political morality is, even today, frequently subject to expediency.

Ports, of course, were notorious for harbouring plague and other infections and Dieppe would have been no exception (Reid, it will be remembered, had instigated some rules of quarantine in Scottish ports). It is quite possible therefore that they all succumbed to one or more such infections.

(There was even a suggestion that Reid died of sorrow at the prospect of the coming Reformation although this was still two years away and not obviously imminent; it would also have been uncharacteristically defeatist. Moreover it could scarcely be said to account for the other deaths.)

Among others affected by the sickness was Lord James Stewart, the prior of St. Andrew's, bastard of James V and known as "Il Bastardo da

Scozia" but he survived the sickness and was present at the bishop's death bed. James Stewart was the illegitimate son of James V and Margaret Erskine, wife of Sir Robert Douglas of Lochleven. Clement VII had dispensed him from the impediments of bastardy so that he could be presented to the Priory of St. Andrew's at the tender age of six or seven, being finally admitted "in commendam" to the temporality ten years later by Paul III. His father and Arran meanwhile enhanced the rents of the priory and themselves took the profits. James Stewart had accompanied the young queen to France in 1548, been a member of the Privy Council from 1550 and, with Reid, been present at the trial of Adam Wallace. In 1550 he obtained the Priory of Pittenweem which he proceeded to dilapidate. Swayed by his teaching, he wrote to John Knox, in 1557, urging him to return to Scotland "in the name of God". Attending the royal wedding, tired of ecclesiastical life, he petitioned the queen for the earldom of Moray. He was offered instead a rich bishopric in France which he declined. In 1559 he was to join the Band of the Congregation and later to become a supporter of the English and to welcome them to Scotland. As earl of Moray he became regent during the minority of James VI and died at the hand of an assassin.

Reid and Lord James had long debated on matters of religion, Lord James putting forward the views of the protestant reformers whilst the bishop held to the catholic faith.

"My lord," the bishop is reported as saying to Lord James[1], knowing that his death was imminent, "Long you and I have been at play for Purgatory; I think that I shall know before long whether there be such a place or not." Lord James then began to exhort the bishop to call to mind the promises of God and the virtues of Christ's death but the bishop replied: "No, my lord, let me alone; you and I never agreed in our life and I think we shall not agree now at my death". It is alleged that knowing the approach of death the bishop had his bed made on or between two coffers and Lord James asked him "why do you lie so? Will you not go to your chamber and not lie here in this common house?" The bishop is then said to have answered: "I am well where I am because I am near my friends." And there he died.

In writing a biography it is possible to assess the character of the subject both from the opinions of those who knew him and from his own writings. We have the opinions of Reid's contemporaries, mostly favourable but we have nothing that he wrote apart from official documents. These last words of his therefore have been given an importance probably far beyond their merit. However they are almost all we have. John Knox, who obtained the account from Lord James, had little time for bishops and regarded "My friends" as referring to the coffers which he supposed were filled with treasures. He implied that the bishop was covetous of his wealth to the end or, worse, idolatrous. This seems, in the light of Reid's conduct generally and his known liberality to others, to have been a most unlikely interpretation of his words. Others have suggested that the coffers contained documents and certainly the bishop had made sure of saving documents from the shipwreck before anything else. It would have been in keeping with his conscientiousness as a state servant to see to their preservation. It would also have been in character for him to have referred to his books as his friends, so that the coffers may have contained some of his literary treasures. On the other hand the suggestion that, by reference to "his friends", he was indicating the coffers, may just have been Lord James mistaken interpretation. The bishop may simply, have wished to remain in the apparently humble lodgings with people who had befriended him in his distress - perhaps folk he had known from previous passage through Dieppe - rather than move to more luxurious lodgings among strangers.

More revealing than this ambiguous reference to 'friends' are the other words attributed to the dying prelate. They suggest a measure of honest doubt, inconsistent with the certainties that the catholic faith had taught him and that he had taught others. It maybe that the last words to Lord James Stewart bear upon one another. Lord James was urging him once again to consider the possibility of conforming, on his death bed, to the new doctrines of the reformers. Reid, however, was too honest to alter his opinions just because his end was near and he was about to find out whether or not he was to experience purgatory. He would not now desert those 'friends' who had looked to him to uphold catholic doctrine.

iii. The last resting place

A descendant of Adam Blackwood, Reid's nephew by marriage, wrote to the dean of Dieppe in 1861 that he had found among his family papers that Reid had been buried in the church of St. Jacques in Dieppe in the chapel of S. Andrew, known as the Scots chapel. It is not known for certain, however, where Robert Reid lies buried for no stone marks the spot, the likelihood still remains that it is in Dieppe where he died, especially had his death been due to an infectious illness.

In 1870 during work on the cemetery of the church of St. Jacques in Dieppe, the floor of the chapel of St. Andrew had to be taken up. There, among a number of bones and skulls were found five coffins lying in a row, four of pine and one of beech wood. In these were five well preserved bodies, which had evidently been embalmed, lying on their backs with their arms folded across their chests. One of them had a few white hairs on his head and a white beard. It was thought that these might well be the remains of the four commissioners together with Sir James Colville of East Wemyss. Lord Fleming, one of the commissioners, may however have died in Paris in which case the fifth coffin could have been that of a retainer. The archives of the region today contain no record of the commissioners' deaths nor of the whereabouts of their remains. However in 1872 following the discovery of the coffins in the chapel of St. Andrew, Abbe Cochet, the inspector of historical monumets in the department of Seine-Inferieur, placed a monumental plaque to the memory of Bishop Robert Reid, in the chapel. It read:

A la Mémoire
de Robert Reid
Evêque d'Orkney (Orcades)
Président du Parlement Ecossais.
Commissaire Député de l'Ecosse
Au mariage de Marie Stuart.
Décédé a Dieppe en Septembre, 1558,
Inhumé dans la Chapelle St. André
dite des Ecossais.
Requiescat in pace.

The chapel of St. Andrew has since been rededicated to the Immaculate Conception and all the memorial tablets, in this chapel, including that to the bishop, (as well as many in the other chapels) have been removed[2]. It is highly probable that the bodies found under the floor of the chapel are indeed those of Bishop Reid and his companions and the great church of St. Jacques is itself a fitting monument to stand above his grave. It is to be regretted that the only memorial to this great prelate and statesman should have been in France and not Scotland and that even that is now no longer to be seen.

iv. The church in Orkney after Reid

Robert Reid was dead. He had fought long and hard for the reform of his church on traditional lines. He had worked to strengthen the framework of the ministry especially in his own diocese and had sought to eradicate the abuses that had been eating away at the church's authority. It had been an uphill struggle with the crown disposing of benefices to unworthy candidates. He was not helped by the fact that he himself was a servant of the crown, that he approved the burning of heretics and that he was the holder of a number of lucrative appointments. It must be said in defence of the latter that his missions for the crown were largely financed out of his own pocket and the income of a bishop of Orkney was one of the smallest of the Scottish prelates. Moreover he had been generous in his lifetime and had cared for many of the less fortunate, providing dowries for girls and education for young men.

Perhaps it was as well that he had died when he did for he never saw the establishment of a religion that he would have found it hard to accept. Gordon Donaldson ('Reformed by Bishops')[3] has pointed out the difference between Reid and his successor, Adam Bothwell. Bothwell became a bishop in the established catholic church but had little hesitation in accepting the Reformation and applying its processes to his diocese. He was, Donaldson maintains, "as typical of the reformed church as Reid had been of the unreformed". That is to say he was a pragmatist as were many in the church at the time. However it must be recalled that Reid had been of necessity pragmatic in all his diplomatic dealings with the English. Faced with the inevitability of a reformed protestant church perhaps he too might have adopted a pragmatic approach. Maybe it is as well that he never had to make that choice. It is possible to believe that he could have lived with Lutheran doctrine and even that of John Calvin, had this became the policy of the government during his lifetime since he was a Scottish patriot as well as a catholic priest. It is difficult however to believe that he could have accepted the Calvinist creed as preached by Knox and his followers. Old age had nevertheless made him more tolerant of the views of others. The horror he had expressed at Wallace's heresies had given way to acceptance of the fact that the prior of St. Andrew's might legitimately hold views that contradicted traditional catholic doctrine.

Donaldson also recalls how Bothwell, by sending the members of the cathedral chapter to minister to the parishes, changed the roles of the diocesan clergy that Reid had so carefully established. That he encountered so little opposition from the clergy leaves one to conjecture that they might have already been expected to adopt this role, in conjunction with their cathedral offices, during the previous administration.

Orkney was fortunate in the choice of a successor to Reid. Perhaps it was also fortunate in the death of its staunchly catholic bishop at such a time. Donaldson's claim that Bothwell was typical of the reformed church is not quite born out by his conduct in Orkney for the islands were less affected by the changes than were most other dioceses throughout Scotland and Donaldson himself admits that the new bishop instituted a reformation more akin to the English than the Scottish one. It was Bothwell who insisted on anointing the infant James VI at his coronation and in whose library no copy of the Book of Common Order was found. It was not the bishop who instigated the prosecution of the provost, Alexander Dick, for saying mass; a provost who did not conform and become a protestant minister until fourteen years after 1560 (although he was 'put to the horn' for non-payment of a third of his benefice that was demanded of clergy who failed to conform). Nor was the provost alone in his reluctance to accept the new order, neither the Archdeacon of Orkney, the Subdean nor the subchanter conformed. The Precentor, Magnus Halcro, became a laird and married his mistress, later being excommunicated for adultery. Although many of the clergy did conform and became ministers or readers in the new church, a greater number did not enter the reformed ministry and little pressure was put on them by the bishop. The parishes do indeed seem to have benefitted nevertheless since, by 1567, all the parishes were being served by either ministers, readers or exhorters, despite the non-conforming views of many of them. It seems that Bothwell was more concerned with the attitude of the laity, on whom he exerted some pressure to attend protestant services, than that of the clergy. It is noteworthy that Shaw in his account of Sixteenth Century Reform ('A Light in the North')[4] writes that "Apart from the clergy which Bothwell brought with him, he found a nucleus of educated and reliable incumbents; this, I am sure, had something to do with the reforms that Robert Reid had brought in about standards of education for certain appointments."

The other manner in which Orkney survived the worst rigours of the Reformation was in the preservation of its cathedral. Where the English Reformation had resulted in a wave of iconoclastic vandalism which had found imitators among the more fanatical Scottish reformers, the Orcadians, who themselves owned their cathedral, ensured that it remained inviolate. Perhaps the statue of Earl Rognvald (if indeed it is he) would have fared better to have remained in the cathedral (if indeed that was where he stood), than have been rendered incognito by wind and weather on Robert Reid's round tower! The legacy of Robert Reid's concern for both the chapter and structure of the church may well have earned the respect of the people of Kirkwall who would have been reluctant to see their most precious monument defaced.

v. Reid's legacy

It was not until six years after his death, that the executors of Reid's will were called upon by the court to confirm his testament, which they did on 4th August 1564. As his legacy tended "to sa gude a fyne and being for the common weill and polecy of the realme", it was the duty of the king to see it accomplished. Mr James MacGill of Nether Rankeillour and Mr. Thomas Maccalzean were the procurators for recovering the 4000 merks owed for the lands of Strathnaver. They and the king's advocate then ordered the three remaining executors, the others having died, to produce the 8000 merks for the Regent and the Privy Council to deposit it in the hands of those who would ensure that the purposes, for which it had been left, were carried out. The three remaining executors were Robert Reid's nephew John, his nephew Walter and schir John Anderson. John Reid and John Anderson hastened to disclaim, by their procurators, that they had ever interfered with the bishops goods and wished to resign as executors. It seems likely that they were aware of the conduct of the third executor, Walter Reid, in his handling of the bishops legacy. In 1576 the regent, James Douglas, earl of Morton, then ordered the one remaining executor, Walter, commendator of Kinloss, to hand over the 8000 merks to the person he appointed to receive it. (It was alleged by John Colville that the regent then punished the executors for supposed crimes and appropriated the money to himself. However it seems that his accusation was a false one and that, on the contrary, Morton ordered the money to be used for the benefit of the country.)

No moneys were forthcoming and, as the years dragged by, Reid's bequest dissolved amidst ineptitude and dishonesty. Most of those concerned were dead before any action was taken. The provost and community of Edinburgh finally commissioned the privy council for an act giving them the power to proceed against Walter, now commendator of Kinloss, for the recovery of the 8000 merks. Two bailies and six burgesses undertook the task of recovering the money and using it for the purposes prescribed in the will. This was in 1582. It then transpired that, of the 4000 marks supposedly in the care of Walter Reid, 1,500 had disappeared and the other 2,500 was in the hands of Anthony Bruce, a burgess of Stirling. The provost and his party, with the commendator of Kinloss attended upon the king, claiming £125.6.8 travelling expenses! The king requested the provost and Walter to recover the 2500 merks from Anthony Bruce and hand it over to the authorities. Eventually. this was paid over in two instalments of 700 and 1800 merks by the year 1587. The remaining 4000 merks owed by McKay for repayment of the mortgage on Strathnaver never materialised. By 1593, after Walter Reid's decease, the provost of Edinburgh accepted the inevitable and declared the town to have been paid "completely"!

Thus Robert Reid's dearest wish was never carried out. He had stipulated for the purchase of Sir John Ramsay's tenement in Edinburgh in which to establish the foundation of a school for teaching children grammar, poetry and oratory and law. A school that was more than a grammar school yet not a university. The act of 1496 had included the establishment of schools of Art and Jure and it doubtless one such as this that Reid had had in mind, since Edinburgh already possessed all the many other types of school then in existence. Where had the money gone? The 4000 merks that had saved McKay from the consequences of his escheat were never repaid; 1500 merks were defrauded by his nephew, Walter, so that ultimately less than one third of the original bequest was applied to any purpose remotely connected with education. In 1587 the teaching of theology was begun at the new university of Edinburgh and, in the same year, that last fraction of Reid's bequest became available to the town of Edinburgh and its university. It is the final irony that the only substantial legacy that the fighter for catholic values left may have been applied to the teaching of protestant theology. Reid's other great interest had been in law, and civil law was not taught at the university until 1710 whilst canon law was no longer relevant in a protestant university. There is therefore no foundation for the belief that bishop Reid of Orkney left money for the founding of the university of Edinburgh, something he neither intended nor particularly desired, whilst his wish to found a school for the young was never fulfilled.

It is doubtful, in any case, as to whether, before the Reformation, as bishop of Orkney, he could have founded a university in Edinburgh which was in the archdiocese of St. Andrew's. St. Andrew's, of course, already had its own university. His own diocese could clearly not support a university and there was already established there a grammar school and a sang school which he had supported and rehoused. If his ambitions for the education of the young of Edinburgh came to nothing at least he had left a legacy in Kirkwall that was to benefit the youth of Orkney for many years to come.

Notes

1. Quoted by Craven: *"History of the Church in Orkney"* vol.i pp.161-2.
2. A facsimile of the plaque erected by Abbe Cochet has recently been donated to the church of St. Jacques by the Orkney Heritage Society and placed in the chapel. Although the title of 'President of the Scottish Parliament' did not exist, Reid had acted as Lord High Commissioner of Parliament, which meant that he had presided over their deliberations and it is therefore not unreasonble for the Abbe to have described him as 'President'.
3. Gordon Donaldson: *"Reformed by Bishops"* p.28
4. Duncan Shaw: "The 16th Century and the Movement for Reform" from Cant & Firth *"The Light in the North"*

Epilogue
Tenebrae

Ecce sacerdos magnus, qui in diebus suis placuit Deo, et inventus est justus, et in tempore iracundiae factus est.

Robert Reid was a man of his time and must be judged as such. It is a regrettable fact that by the sixteenth century the catholic church had, in many respects, ceased to practice what its founders had preached. There were those who tried hard to restore the credibility of their church and to reform its institutions from within. Too often they were defeated by those to whom the church was a comfortable haven in which to further their own interests; by ignorance; and by the secular rulers who saw their interests best served by control of their clerical hierarchy.

At the very time that integrity of the church's leaders in Scotland was being questioned there were, returning from the continent, men who had been studying at universities in Europe that were coming under the increasing influence of the protestant reformers. From Germany, there came also the invention of printing with movable type. Suddenly ideas need no longer be the prerogative of the monastic orders and the universities; books that had been painstakingly copied by hand became readily available to all who could read. In addition the Bible, became available in the vernacular. Men could read the scriptures for themselves and could question the interpretation of them that had, for so long, been made for them by the church. The epistles of St. Paul, especially, had a profound influence on the reformers.

In Scotland even the poorest and least educated were not blind to the failings of the church. Sir David Lyndsay, a loyal servant of the crown and pillar of the 'establishment', who had been tutor to the young James V and Lord Lyon King at Arms, put their thoughts into words, wonderfully capturing the mood of the times in his 'Ane Pleasant Satyr of the Thrie Estaitis'. His Pardoner, who sells indulgences, is dependent upon the superstitions of the ignorant. He clearly has a grudge against both the reformers for decrying the selling of indulgences and the translators of the Bible who allow men to read the words of St. Paul. He says to the poorman:

> "...I gif to the devill, with gud entent,
> This unsell wickit New Testament,
> With thame that it translattit:
> Pardonaris gettis no cheretie,
> Withowt that thay debait it...
> ...Bot now, allace! our grit abusioun
> Is cleirly knawin to our confusioun,
> Quhilk I may sair repent:
> Off all the creddence now am I quyte,
> Ilk man hes me now at dispyte,
> That reidis the New Testament.
> Duill fall to thame that it has wrocht,
> Swa sall thame that the buik hame brocht,
> Als I pray to the Rude
> That Martyne Luter, that fails loan
> Black Bullinger and Melancthoun
> Had bene smorde in thair cude.
> I wald Sanct Pawle had neuir bene borne;
> And als I wald his buikis
> War nevir red into the kirk,
> Bot amang friers into the mirk;
> Or riven amang the ruikis."[1]

The pauper however has few illusions:

> "Our Bishops, with their lustie rokats quhyte,
> They flow in riches royallie, and delyte.
> Lyke paradice bene thair palices and places;
> And wants na pleasour of the fairest faces.
> Als thir prelates hes great perogatryves;
> For quhy? Thay may depairt ay with thair wyves,
> Without ony correctioun of damage;
> Syne tak ane uther wantoner, but marriage.
> But doubt I wald think it ane pleasant lyfe,
> Ay on, quhen I list, to part with my wyfe,
> Syne tak an uther of far greater beutie :
> But ever, alace, my lords, that may not be!
> For I am bund in marriage;
> Bot thay lyke rams, rudlie in thair rage,
> Unpysalt rinnis amang the sillie yowis,

Sa lang as kynde of nature in them growis. "[2]

Abbots fare no better in the view of 'Chastitie':

Chastitie: "My lords, this abbot and this Priores
They scorne thair gods; this is my reason quhy,
Thay beare and habite of feinyiet halines,
And in thair deid thay do the contrary.
For to live chaist thay vow solemnitly:
Bot fra that thay be sikker of thair bowis,
Thay live in huirdome and in harlotry.
Examine them ,Sir, how thay observe their vowis. "

All of which the abbot himself confirms!

"Tuiching my office I say to yow plainlie,
My monk and I we leif richt easilie;
Thair is na monks, from Carrick to Carraill,
That fairs better, and drinks mair helsum aill.
My Prior is ane man of great devotioun,
Thairfoir daylie he gets and doble portioun". [3]
Toward the end of the play 'Diligence' proclaims:
"It is devysit be thir prudent Kingis,
Correctioun, and King Humanitie,
That thair Leigis, induring all their ringis,
With the avyce of the Estaitis Thrie,
Sall manfullie defend and fortifie
The Kirk of Christ, and his religioun,
Without dissimulance or hyocrisie,
Under the pain of their punitioun".

and then pronounces to the Thrie Estaitis how the church may be reformed.[4] Alas the vested interests of that most powerful of the estates, the clergy, prevented their acting as 'Diligence' demanded and led to their suffering 'their punitioun'.

That Lyndsay's analysis was not exaggerated is evident from characters of most of the bishops who were in place in Robert Reid's time. To start with only three were priests, the rest were deacons, monks or in minor orders; six of them were under thirty years of age. They were nearly all desirous of obtaining opulent benefices rather than having the ambition to be pastors of their flock. Many, and Reid was among them, became state dignitaries. The following description of a number of them indicates to what depth the church had sunk in its upper echelons:

'One was a deserter of his flock; three were invaders of religious houses and rioters; one a monster of profligacy and a bastard monger; twenty two others were concubinary bishops; three were formal traitors and other "good Englishmen"; one was a thief, embezzling the treasury of the realm and two were squanderers dilapitating their bishoprics'.

All these things were common knowledge among the laity. Overweening pride and greed must have blinded many of the senior clergy to the damage they were inflicting on the church they had been called to serve. Some however sensed the approaching storm and, like desperate men, lashed out at the 'heretics' but, like those who attempt to ward off a swarm of bees, they only succeeded in antagonising their foes still further and ended in being stung to death. Such indeed was the fate of Cardinal Beaton.

Nevertheless, despite the clouds that were gathering over the church in Scotland, there were still some few bright candles flickering in the gloom. Such a light was Robert Reid. As a lawyer he was a stern judge, consenting to the burning of heretics, as his church demanded, but trusted to give fair judgement in the many civil disputes and arbitrations he was called on to deliver. Although he insisted that his pupils should receive a legal training at a "flourishing university" such as Orleans, Louvain, Bourges, Paris or Poitiers, he himself, may not ever have been formally qualified in law nor held any degree as a Doctor of Law. Nevertheless, as a practical lawyer, he was outstanding, and this fact was acknowledged when he was chosen as a member of the College of Justice and later as its President. Reid's concerns for the education of the young have already been shown. With Giovanni Ferrerio's help he made the Monastery of Kinloss into a minor university for the monks. He brought other monks from the Priory of Beauly to Kinloss to further their education. As bishop he refounded both the grammar school and sang school in Orkney. He spent his private fortune on educating his nephews and other young men in Paris and acted as tutor to others. The queen herself received religious instruction from Robert Reid. That his legacy, consisting of the bulk of his fortune, for the founding of a school for young men in Edinburgh, was never applied to the cause so dear to his heart, was no fault of the bishop's.

A scholar, a lover and a collector of books, Reid greatly expanded the library at Kinloss. As one of his monks wrote: "Ceainly in short he prefers nothing ever to the best books; the more he brings volumes of better letters of all kinds and the best of them to this place diligently and every day, sparing no expenditure, the fewer he has, as he is accustomed always to say openly in the presence of the learned men and he is of this opinion".

Reid has no literary works of his own to his credit although there are two that have erroneously been ascribed to him. One was a History of the Orkney Isles compiled for the King of Denmark, a manuscript copy of which was in the bishop's possession and the other a manuscript genealogy of the family of Sinclair which Reid sent to the Danish king.

As a statesman and diplomat he he may not have been in the class of Cardinal Beaton, nor did he aim to be. Beaton had ambitions to lead the nation and was a diplomat of brilliance. He succeeded in both roles and paid the price. Robert Reid's ambitions were more modest, those of a servant rather then a master. A loyal Scot, he supported Beaton's policy of independence from England but was prepared to be pragmatic in his approach. As long as there was a threat from the England of Henry VIII he stood firmly on the side of the cardinal, though always ready to seek peace if it could be obtained with honour. After Beaton's assassination and when a new monarch was on the English throne, he was prepared to be more flexible in his dealings with the 'auld enemy'. During the reign of Henry the eighth he paid four diplomatic visits to England and subsequently one visit each to both Edward VI and Mary. Obtaining for himself a reputation as a skilled negotiator and as a man of integrity, he was treated with respect by all three monarchs. He also helped to renegotiate the treaty with East Friesland.

Loyal at all times to his monarch he was never a close confident of James V, despite the many missions he undertook on his behalf. It was with the young queen Mary that he came closest to the throne and whom he served with devotion from the time of her accession to her wedding at the age of fifteen. When she was six years old he was given the responsibility of finding a doctor for her and, on her reaching the age of eleven, he acted as her procurator when she discharged the duke of Chatelherault as regent in favour of her mother. If he did not live to see her crowned queen of France neither did he have to witness her rejection by her people and her flight to England.

Twice he visited France in connection with royal marriages and, at the wedding of the queen, he was one of the leaders of the Scottish commission and dealt firmly with the unreasonable demands that the French king made after the wedding. Some were to maintain that that firmness cost him his life.

Reid's diplomatic skills were not only displayed on foreign embassies. At home he acted as peacemaker between the cardinal and the governor and between the latter and the earl of Lennox, possibly preventing civil war. As a loyal son of the church he felt it his duty to support his archbishop and cardinal and when Beaton was imprisoned, although elected to the governor's secret council, he paid a visit to his archbishop in his confinement. Later when the governor was "deposed" he was invited to join the new council. Although unable to reconcile the two archbishops whose pride prevented them from enjoying mutual respect, he was the obvious choice to adjudicate on the reprehensible fracas between their supporters before the cathedral of Glasgow.

On four occasions he was chosen to be a member of the Privy Council. Whilst abbot of Kinloss he was a regular attendant in parliament, being appointed a parliamentary commissioner on a number of occasions and three times he was chosen as one of the Lord of the Articles, a rare privelege for a mere abbot. As bishop he attended less often but was again twice a Lord of the Articles and on at least two occasions Lord High Commissioner, presiding over the parliament. In financial affairs he was frequently in demand as auditor of accounts; twice he was commissioner for letting crown lands and once for the introduction of standard measures. He was responsible for introducing quarantine measures at Scottish ports and for restricting Scottish currency from going abroad.

Despite all the work he undertook for the state, Reid did not ignore the needs of either his abbey or his diocese. He was concerned to restore a vibrant life to the community of both abbey and cathedral and to extend and beautify their material structures. Nor was this done to the neglect of his congregations, he was always ready to advise, adjudicate and at times to aid financially those who came to him for succour. His one failing as a bishop was that he spent too little time in his diocese. In all he paid five visits to Orkney never staying long before being called away on state business. Bishops on the mainland of Scotland, especially those with lowland sees, could obey the call of their sovereign or parliament and remain within reach of their dioceses. For a bishop in the isles it was not so simple a matter and others in similar positions experienced the same difficulty. It could be argued that an important public servant should not have been placed in such a situation and should have refused the preferment when offered. However bishoprics were often given to statesmen in order to enhance their standing, especially among foreign dignitaries and a refusal would have been unthinkable to an ambitious man, which Reid certainly was. In the circumstances he took every means he could to ensure that the life of the diocese was entrusted to men who would conduct its affairs as he would have done himself, and that the service of the church was maintained with regularity and dignity.

Although he would seem to have been a good judge of men and to have made sound choices in his companions and subordinates both at Kinloss and Kirkwall, it is sad to think that two of the men in whom he put most trust should have had cause to quarrel with one another. Giovanni Ferrerio, whom he brought to Kinloss to teach the monks, was a scholar with the same hunanist sympathies as the bishop, and a devout catholic, and Adam Elder was a man to whom Reid trusted the care and instruction of his nephew and successor. Despite Reid's regard for both of them, or perhaps because of it, they seem to have had little regard for one another.

The moral turpitude of the Scottish bishops at this time has been remarked upon. Denied by their church the right to marry, many of them kept mistresses quite openly. Some, like Cardinal Beaton and Marion Ogilvy, had a permanent alliance and lived virtually as man and wife, producing offspring who were all able to obtain favourable positions in life due to their patrimony. Others, like Patrick Hepburn of Moray, who is said to have had eleven children by three different women, were more promiscuous. None felt or showed any shame for their behaviour and took little trouble to disguise it. Bishop Reid had no mistress. That may seem a bold statement to make in the climate of the age but, had he had one, there is no doubt that history would have recorded it. Biographers now-a-days are much concerned with the sexuality of their subjects and it might be asked as to whether a celibate bishop in sixteenth century Scotland could be other than homosexual. Reid was much in the company of young men and was concerned to see both his monks and his friends children receive a good education and to undertake tutoring them himself on occasions. One can make what one likes of this but it is slender evidence for assuming him to be homosexual and there is no scandal known to be associated with him as either abbot or bishop. In the end the question is an irrelevance and also a slur on all those devout christians who see service to God as sufficiently fulfilling for all their needs.

Although in Robert Reid the church in Scotland had a man who brought honour to an institution that seemed to be intent on self destruction and served faithfully a monarchy whose actions often lent aid to that process, he was no saint. Too many of the failings that beset the age in which he lived he accepted unquestioningly; nepotism, plurality, the acceptance of great divergences in wealth and the burning of heretics. With the latter he may have been hypocritical in that, like so many of those in power, he regarded the burning of heretics as acceptable in the case of the poor and ignorant, such as Adam Wallace, but was prepared to overlook the 'heretical' opinions of such highborn characters as James Stewart. On the other hand his views on heresy may have undergone a change as he studied the works of the reformers and discussed their views with his friend Ferrerio. However those failings, which were common currency of the times, should not detract from the very real virtues that caused him to stand out from the crowd of profligate churchmen whose selfishness was bringing about the destruction of the church to which he had devoted his life.

Dying as he did, after the triumph of the royal wedding and before the reign of catholicism in Scotland came to an end, it might be thought that Robert Reid's life had been one of successful achievement. Yet almost all his achievements were to prove fleeting ones. The two royal weddings, with which he had been concerned, were short lived. James V's first wife died within weeks of her arrival in Scotland; Mary, married in 1558, became queen of France on the death of Henry II in 1559 and was widowed in 1560.

Reid's abbey of Kinloss passed to the care of his nephew, Walter, who subscribed to the Covenant in 1560 and alienated much of the lands of both Kinloss and Beauly. Walter later married Margaret Collace by whom he had several children and who, on Walter's death, came to possess the abbey. Thereafter she was in dispute with Edward Bruce, parson of Torrie and later Lord Kinloss, her husband's cousin, who had obtained the fishing rights and who now claimed to be called the abbot of Kinloss.

Both the abbey of Kinloss and the priory of Beauly are now in ruins and Reid's new buildings served the monks and the church he loved for few years after his demise. Today there is little to recall the abbey's former glory. A few scattered walls and ruined buildings stand, or lie, beside the village of Kinloss. A new wall encloses much that remains (although Reid's tower dwelling stands without) and within it the grass is neatly mown. Graves stones and funerary monuments drift between the ruins recalling the dead of more recent centuries. On the far side of the abbey buildings stand orderly rows of identical gravestones each bearing the name and rank of a fallen airman from the last war, mostly from the Royal Canadian Airforce. How does the shade of Abbot Crystal look upon these companions of the hallowed ground and does Abbot Robert return from his rest in Dieppe to lament the state of his fine library? Perhaps, but Robert Reid might well enjoy the company of those young Canadians whose spirits throng the ground where once more serious minded novices walked the cloisters and recited their novenas. Giovanni Ferrerio too might like to spend some time in eternity passing on his wisdom to the young minds so abruptly taken from this mortal world. It is a peaceful place and one where bishop, abbot, scholar and airmen could rest harmoniously together.

The ruins of the Priory, in the centre of the small town of Beauly, have also been well cared for and, unlike those of Kinloss, the walls of the abbey church remain largely intact although roofless. Here too there have been burials in recent years though none of the armed forces. The lawns around the ruins are smoothly mown and trees, several old and large, give shade to the living and those at rest. Monsieur Lubias, who maybe lies beneath that very grass, would be content with the care that has been taken of the grounds of both Beauly and Kinloss although there are now no traces of his beloved fruit trees.

Much of Reid's collection of books has survived and many can be found in the libraries of all the four ancient Scottish universities. However they have few readers now-a-days beyond scholarly researchers in medieval latin. (Appendix 2)

Reid's diocese of Orkney remained in catholic hands for barely a year after his death. His successor Adam Bothwell, who accepted the Reformation, sent members of the chapter to minister to the parishes and although some stalwart catholics remained true to the faith of their forefathers, both among clergy and laity, most accepted the new ways, finding little alteration to their lives apart from the dropping of the mass. One or two found this latter insupportable and in the words of Edward Sinclair "wald in na sort consent the mass wor doune".

If Reid did indeed add to the length of the cathedral nave then, for many years of protestant worship there, his efforts were wasted, for the body of the kirk was partitioned off and services held only at the east end. His palace is now a ruin and even the statue that he placed on the tower is so worn away as to be unrecognisable and subject to the conjectures of historians and archaeologists.

The church of St. Olaf which he restored was abandoned and made use of for a variety of secular purposes. Only a doorway now remains. Another church of that name was built at the end of the nineteenth century for use by the Episcopal Church of Scotland thus retaining a link with an episcopate.

Although his and Cardinal Beaton's efforts to keep the English out of Scottish affairs had succeeded in his lifetime, when the English queen, Elizabeth, died in 1603, James VI of Scotland became James I of England and a century later the two countries became one.

The fate of Robert Reid's legacy for the founding of a school has already been examined.

So it might be assumed that Robert Reid had largely lived his life in vain. It would be a false assumption. Regardless of what develops in the future the life of a man who keeps the faith, cares for others and seeks to leave the world in which he lived in a better state than he found it, has not lived in vain. Reid was loved and honoured by those who knew him and respected by those with whom he had official dealings whether friend or enemy.

After he had left Kinloss to become bishop of Orkney, one of his monks wrote of him:"Now among the guiders of souls I am calling by name you, Robert, the most watchful shepherd sowing the word of God in his bishopric of Orkney though you are far away from us now in your episcopate watching over your flock and discharging strenuously and sedulously the ministry committed to you by Lord God... those who knew you intimately agree with me that you shrink from, are more completely foreign to and devoid of, those vices and filth which I related a little before... And you show it with words and example, so scanty in these times of ours, namely with erudition, morals and entire life, to great joyfulness and delight not only of your own soul but also of the souls of your sheep... I know you wish greatly that your virtues and all merits should be rather concealed and lurk in your own consciousness rather than be known by anyone's laudation. Moreover this wise and blameless man sees and considers earnestly that the honours of this world, riches, dignities and the many other temporal things that fell to his lot but, always mindful of death and of the account to be given to the supreme judge, he has not the use of them all, as received by the lord from this world but, by the servant and good manager, from God. Indeed he does not take pride in honours nor is puffed up, does not set his mind on pouring riches, by no means grows insolent with fortunate success in affairs, is not made blind with dignities and other temporal gifts... He does not esteem the remaining riches how great soever; not the castles, not palaces, though they are appropriate to the most magnificent bishop... not gold, not silver, not fields, not horses, not attire, not jewels. Briefly and certainly does he not prefer anything to best books."

George Mackenzie in his 'Writers of the Scots Nation'[5] records that Adam Elder, who was close to Reid and tutor to his nephew, Walter, said of him in a sermon in which he compared him to St. Bernard: "He was one of the most eloquent persons of his age, either on the bench or in the pulpit, being always agreeable, instructive and nervous in his reasonings; his exhortations were pressing, his admonitions serious, and his threatenings, tho' they were accompanied with inexpressible vehemence and force, yet were tempered with meekness, that it plainly appeared to everyone that it was nothing of a chagriness of temper or an insulting and domineering humour, but for the instruction and salvation that made him do it. That he was a severe disciplinarian; that no man in the age he lived in, knew the civil and canon law better than he did; that he was charitable beyond expression."

To the bishop's nephew, Walter, Elder added: "For it is not necessary to enumerate for you the other numerous works of charity in which his beneficence is employed as, for example, respecting the starvation of the poor and oppressed, which has been going on for years, food for the body, a pious easing of burdens, an honourable placing in marriage of girls whose fortunes are too small to provide them with dowries, and a most generous nurture of many young hearts in literary studies…

Indeed, finally, he never rates anything more highly than very good books; and more, he diligently amasses here more of the finest volumes of every kind of superior literature, without regard for cost, the less he is always accustomed to think of himself and to say openly in front of the learned. There are many things of this kind, but it would take too long to go through them".

Adam Elder also composed the following verses in Latin in praise of his mentor, Robert Reid. (Wallace has a version of the poem in English in his 'Islands of Orkney' published in 1698[6]. The following translation is by Dr. Maxwell-Stuart of St. Andrew's University).

> *Why should I try to touch with a narrow poem upon the praises,*
> *which no power of eloquence can celebrate?*
> *You are famous for eloquence, Bishop most worthy of Heaven.*
> *You spring from an ancient nobility of race,*
> *and you look after the flock committed to your care, and you raise up*
> *   the person lying down,*
> *leading them to better things by your example;*
> *and just as the rising sun scatters shadows from the earth,*
> *you throw light upon blind hearts with your rays.*

You encourage the dilatory, you rebuke, you censure everyone
who falls headlong into evil, people whom ancient terror drives.
Your house is open to the poor, your will is quick to act,
and your right hand is always bountiful to the good.
No one better keeps wolves away from the sacred sheepfolds,
so that they may not savage or snatch away the flock of Christ.
Therefore because of your great devout studies and hard work,
may the God of peace grant you to enjoy peace.
May He grant that everything turn out well for your prayers,
and a good wind help your successes.

There is no doubt, both from his actions and from the words of those close to him, that Reid stood head and shoulders above most of his fellow bishops, both in erudition and morals. He tried to raise the catholic church from the low esteem in which it had sunk, to reform its processes and to keep at bay the approaching tide of protestant reform. He had too few allies with sufficient moral authority to give him support. Perhaps also he was himself too much diverted from the task by the calls on his time and abilities by secular affairs.

Would Scotland have avoided the austerities of the Reformation and remained a catholic country had other churchmen followed the bishop of Orkney's example? It is a question to which there is now no answer but it is most likely that the seeds had been sown before ever Reid became a force in the land. If indeed there had been more like him it is possible that reform from within might have delayed that from without but, in the end, Scotland was surely soil ripe for the cultivation of Calvinism.

Leo Nowisilski[6] in his thesis on the Life and Times of Robert Reid sums up the character of the man who was, but for one year of bishop Bothwell's episcopacy, the last Roman Catholic bishop of Orkney:

"A man of inborn talents, wise, sagacious, generous to such an extent that he benefited all places of his secular and church activities; a many sided man infused with culture, enlightened and learned in advance of his time at least in his country, accomplished; judicious builder, religious in architecture and fine arts; experienced and remarkable in many respects, he obtained a pile of offices: politician, lawyer of great celebrity, eminent prelate and churchman with unity of faith and knowledge and no divorce between God and the world. A Christian in a world where even bishops were sceptic in religion and indifferent to the church, a Catholic in an age of Reformation, an aesthete in a universe from which beauty seems to have disappeared" (this is surely to ignore the flowering of art and learning produced by the Renaissance of the 15th and 16th centuries). "A man of irreproachable character and conspicuous virtues in that immoral, licentious age; an idealist with boundless loyalty, fidelity and great devotion to duty in the era of traitors. Not a man of ancient and honourable lineage, but an aristocrat in spirit; not an ingenious creator of new systems, not an excellent scholar prolific of original works but an enthusiastic and scrupulous collector of opinions of various authors; not a fiery preacher or profound theologian but one who lived the life of the entire nation - ideo fecit illum Dominus crescere in plebem suam - such was Reid. Soon after his death the changes in religion in Scotland prevented any evidence leading to canonization if even proofs of sanctity existed; therefore, though we know nothing of Reid's vices we are bound to say: he was not a Saint; but we cannot share Knox's misgivings that Reid departed his life "wither, the great day of the Lord will declare"; because Robert Reid spent his life serving his neighbour in works of public purposes and died in harness of national service as the last bright ray of the Church that shone over independent Scotland, as the last scion of that remote hierarchy which blessed the brave warriors and their king for Bannockburn."

It is hard to quarrel with this assessment although, as a catholic priest and member of a religious order, this biographer may, in his enthusiasm, have been over generous to his subject. Certainly Robert Reid was no saint but he was hard working, generous and just and, in his era, a man of outstanding virtue.

All in all, whatever his failings, there is no doubt that Orkney can be proud of the priest and Scotland of the man.

Notes

1. Sir David Lindsay: *"Ane Pleasant Satyr of the Thrie Estaitis"*. Act III.Sc2.
2. Ibid. Act III Sc.7.
3. Ibid. Act IV Sc.3.
4. Ibid. Act IV Sc.6
5. George Mackenzie: *"Writers to the Scottish Nation"* vol.iii, p. 50
6. Nowosilski p.261-2.

Appendix 1
Letters from two popes

1. Pope Clement VII to Robert Reid, 26th November 1523

Clement etc. to his dear son Robert Reid, clerk of the diocese of St. Andrews, Master of Arts, greeting, etc.

It accords with reason and is consistent with honesty that, in the case of death overcoming the Roman Pontiff and his letters being left incomplete, this document be issued as having his authority. Seeing that our predecessor, Pope Hadrian VI of happy memory, was for some time previously willing to look favourably on you and grant you his good will, since you had been commended to him on many occasions for your knowledge of letters, your honesty of life and morals, and your other merits of probity and virtue; and absolving you now and for the future from any sentences of excommunication, suspension, and any other ecclesiastical penalties you have incurred in any way, as far as this agrees with the effect of the things underwritten;

and further more assessing each and every ecclesiastical benefice with cure which you were occupying, and those with or without cure which you were expecting, and in addition those in which and to which you possessed the right, (whatever, however many, and of whatsoever kind they were), and the true annual values of their fruits, reversals and incomes;

and having regard to your specific supplications on this matter, was inclined immediately before the [following] date, i.e. 31st January in the first year of his pontificate, to grant you whichever two cures or otherwise incompatible ecclesiastical benefices simultaneously, (even if they be the parish church), or their vicarial duties in perpetuity or dignities, minor dignities, administrations or offices in metropolitan or collegiate cathedrals, and dignities in metropolitan cathedrals of belonging to the greater bishoprics, or in the principal collegiate churches of this kind, or any combination of these, and which have a cure of souls attached;

if they were otherwise canonically conferred upon you, or you were elected, presented, or otherwise assumed to them or installed in them; [he granted that] you might receive and retain both together for as long as you lived, and dispose of them together or seperately, simply or in exchange, as many times as you wished; and in place of office or offices so disposed of, you might receive another similar or dissimilar ecclesiastical benefice, or no more than two other similar or dissimilar likewise incompatible ecclesiastical benefices together for as long as you lived, (as is mentioned previously), provided you were willing to retain the lawful valuations assigned thereto by the General Council;

and he graciously granted dispensation, as a particular favour, from any other Apostolic decrees and appointments with regard to churches in which there might be incompatible benefices of this kind, from statutes reinforced by oath, Apostolic confirmation, or any other surety, and from customs and anything else not contrary to Apostolic authority, on condition that the incompatible benefices of this kind be not deprived of the offices which are due to them, and a cure of souls be not attached to them;

We wish to put them into effect, and We declare by the said authority that the present letters are sufficient plainly to confirm the absolution and dispensation of this kind in any place whatever, and that no corroborative evidence be required to confirm them a second time.

Let no one be permitted in any way to invalidate or rashly dare to oppose this document issued by Our will and decree. If anyone, however, presumes to make such an attempt, let him know he will have incurred the anger of Almighty God and of the blessed apostles, Peter and Paul.

Given at Rome at St. Peter's, 26th November 1523, in the first year [of Our pontificate].

2. Pope Clement VII to Robert Reid, 22nd August 1525

Clement etc. to his beloved son Robert Reid, perpetual vicar of the parish church of Kirkaldy in the dioces of St. Andrews, Master of Arts, greeting etc.

The knowledge of letters and honesty of life and morals and other laudable merits of proberty and virtue for which you have been commended to Us as a person worthy of trust, lead Us now, freely and as an act of grace, to render to you all ecclesiastical benefices with or without cure which have been vacant for some time already and are in the gift of the Holy See; and we have reserved to Ourselves the bestowal and disposition of those which will be vacant henceforth, relying upon no matter what authority, knowingly or ignorantly, to call this in question;

Since, therefore, it has happened that the office of perpetual vicar of the parish of Kirkcaldy in the diocese of St. Andrews, by the free resignation of Our beloved son Robert Shanwell, recently perpetual vicar of this church, as a result of the post he obtained from Our dear son John Thornton, clerk of the said diocese, and the proctor especially appointed by him for this purpose, and [the resignation] having been freely laid in Our hands and by Us sent to the aforesaid See;

the office has been made vacant and will be vacant for the time being; We, by reservation [of the offie] and by decree, the abovesaid offering no impediment thereto, agree to your longstanding request that you may receive and retain for as long as you live any two cures or otherwise simultaneously incompatible ecclesiastical benefices, even if they are parish churches, or their vicarial dues in perpetuity, or dignities, minor dignities, administrations, or offices in metropoitan or collegiate cathedrals; and dignities in metropoitan cathedrals belonging to the greater bishoprics, or principal collegiate churches, or any combination of these: and with respect to the dignities, lesser dignities, administrations or offices of this kind which are usually assumed by election or which has a cure of sous attached, if they are otherwise conferred on you canonically, these you have a dispensation to receive and retain as long as you live, and to dispose of them together or collectively, as many times as you wish;

and in place of the office or offices so disposed of receive another similar or dissimilar ecclesiastical benefice together for as long as you live, provided you are willing to retain the values assigned thereto by Apostolic authority.

You may also hold the subdeanery of the Moray church, although the greater dignity attached thereto is not in the hands of the bishop, and, by the said dispensation, the vicarial duties in perpetuity of the church of Garntully and Drumgeldy of the same diocese. These among others you may hold in recognitionof your aforesaid merits, since We wish to grant you a particular favour; and We absolve you now and for the future from whatever sentences of excommunication, suspension, interdict, and any other ecclesiastical sentences, censures, and penalties imposed on you by right or by man on whatever occasion and for whatever reason, if any have been imposed on you in any way, as far as this agrees wuith the effect of these present letters;

and We assess each and every ecclesiastical benefice with or without cure which you hold, and every ecclesiastical benefice with or without cure which you expect, in which and to which you are in any way entitled by right, whatever, however many, and of whatever kind they may be; and having accurate, up-to-date assessments of the aforesaid fruits, rents, and incomes of the subdeanery and the said vicarage, the said vicarage's fruits, rents, and incomes being worth, according to their general annual estimate, 18 pounds sterling, as you also claim, whether by the aforesaid assessment or by any other way;

either as the result of the resignation of some other person, or by the similar resignation of the said Robert or of someone else from [the vicarage], made freely in the Roman Curia, or outwith it, or in front of a public notary and witnesses; or according to the constitution of Pope John XXII, Our predecessor of happy memory, which begins, 'Execrabilis'; or through the puruit of another ecclesiastical benefice left vacant by whatsoever authority - even if it has been left vacant for such a long time that its transfer has legally devolved upon this see, according to the statutes of the Lateran Council - the aforesaid vicarage has been reserved particularly or otherwise generally to Apostolic disposition. Some people are disputing that in a lawsuit, whose standing We wish to have reserved to Ourself, and for the moment the question remains undecided.

But provided disposition of that post, with all its rights and appurtanences, belong to Us on this occasion, by Apostolic authority, We confer it upon you; and We provide further Our decision that it is invalid and idle for anyone, relying on any authority whatever, knowingly or ignorantly, to call this in question. It will be considered an attempt to call this in question if, at some point up till now or at any time henceforth the contrary constitutions of Our predecessor PopeBoniface VIII of pious memory, and other Apostolic constitutions notwithstanding, anyone had made or will make provision for himself regarding ecclesiastical benefices of this kind, or other ecclesiastical benefices in that region, by obtaining special or general letters from his See or its legates; and if by meansof those letters or by any other means the result has been prohibition, reservation, and decree.

In pursuit of the aforesaid vicarage We wish to give you precedence over all other such [other claimants], provided this does not give rise to any injustice to them in their pursuit of other benefices;

Or if, in the case of presentation of a suitable person by the Archbishop himself to the aforesaid vicarage during its temporary vacancy, and in the case of such presentation according to ancient approved practice and thus far peacefully observed custom, it is claimed as a privilege by Our venerable brother, the Archbishop of St. Andrews, Our dear sons of the Abbey and conventual monastery of Dunfermline of the Order of St. Benedict of the same diocese, or by anyone else commonly or seperately from the said See, that they are in no way bound, and cannot be compelled, to receive or provide for anyone; and with respect to the bestowal, provision, presentation, or any other disposition, conjoined or seperately, of ecclesiastical benefices of this kind, or any other ecclesiastical benefices, to those who are looking for them; it is of no avail to be provided with Apostolic letters which do not make full, express, and word for word mention of this kind of privilege; and whatever other indulgence of the said See exists, general or particular, and of whatever wording, in which the privilege is not expressly mentioned, or mentioned in full, the effect of this kind of favour is in every way impeded or deferred, and the entire stipulation concerning it must be considered to be in Our present letters.

We make particular mention that, together with the aforesaid subdeanery and the vicarage you have obtained, or with whatever other two incompatible ecclesiastical benefices you have obtained by force of the said dispensation for the time being, We grant dispensation by the wording of these present letters, as a mark of particular favour, to receive and retain for as long as you live the aforesaid vicarage and some other third cure or otherwise incompatible ecclesiastical benefice, even if it is a parish, or its vicarial dues in perpetuity, or the dignity, minor dignity, administration, or office in a metropolitan or collegiate cathedral, and the dignity in a cathedral belonging to a greater bishopric, or a principl collegiate church of this kind; and with respect to the dignity, lesser dignity, admiistration, or office of this kind which is usually assumed by election and which has a cure of souls attached, if it is otherwise conferred on you canonically, or you are elected, presented, or otherwise assmed to it and installed therein;

and this you may dispose of simply or in exchange, as many times as you wish, and in place of the office so disposed of receive another similar or dissimilar ecclesiastical benefice; or a third cure, or otherwise similarly incompatible ecclesiastical benefice; and provided that among these three incompatible ecclesiastical benefices there are not more than two parish churches or perpetual vicarial dues at the same time as long as you live, you may keep them freely and licitly, according to the constitutions of the General Council, and whatever other constitutions and Apostolic ordinances of the Church which may refer to a third incompatible benefice of this kind; and statutes reinforced by oath, Apostolic confirmation, or any other surety; and customs, and anything else not contrary to the said Apostolic authority.

We grant this, provided that the vicarage that has been resigned, and any third incompatible benefice of this kind, be not deprived of the offices which are owed to it; and that the cure of souls attached to the vicarage which has been resigned and to the aforesaid incomatible benefices be not neglected in any way.

Let no one be permitted to infringe or rashly dare to oppose this decree of Our absolution, grant, provision, decreed will,and dispensation. If anyone, however, presumes to make such an attempt, let him know he will have incurred the anger of Almighty God and of the blessed Apostles, Peter and Paul.

Given at Rome at St. Peter's, 26th November 1525, in the second year [of Our pontificate.]

3. Pope Clement VII to Robert Reid, 4th July 1528

Clement etc. to his dear son Robert Reid, Abbot of the Monastry of Kinloss, of the Cistercian Order, in the diocese of Moray, greeting etc.

The careful povidence of the Apostolic See for those who wish to led the monastic life so that they may be able to fulfil their pious intentions to the praise of God has been accustomed to maintain an Apostolic watchfulnesss, and willingly bestows great pains on the properous and devoted care of the state of all its churches and monasteries; and so that you may not suffer the inconveniences of a long vacancy, it swiftly comes to their aid by providing a remedy.

For some time now We have reserved the appointments of all the churches and monasteries, vacant then and vacant before, in the aforesaid See, to our decision and disposition, and We deckare that it is invalid and idle for anyone, relying on any authority whatsoever, knowingly or ignorantly, to call this in question.

Therefore since at this time the monastery of Kinloss of the Cistercian Order in the diocese of Moray, of which Our dear son Thomas, recently abbot of this monastery, had the rule and administration, has been freely and willingly delivered into Our hands by John Thornton, clerk of the diocese of St. Andrews, the proctor especially appointed by him for this purpose, first of all We issue a warning that no abbot of the said Order who has been put in charge of a monastery by licence and consent of the General Chapter of this Order, can resign in any way the privileges and Apostolic indults granted by Us to the aforesid Cistercian Order, under penalty of a general sentence of excommunication by so doing; and by the same resignation, both he and the aforesaid vacant monastery will have incurred forfeitures, unless such a resignation has been placed in the hands of the Roman Pontiff for the time being, and acknowledgement by him in secret consistory, provided that on this occasion We have proposed that the resignation be acknowledged, and the aforesaid See agrees the position has been vacated and is vacant at the time; and as We have heard that you wish to serve the Lord of virtues in the said monastery, united with Our dear sons in the monastic life, because of the reward of a better life, We wish to nurture you in this your laudable intention and make provision for the same monastery, which no one but Ourself could or can do; by reservation and decree, the abovesaid notwithstanding, so that the monastery be not exposed to the inconveniences of a long vacancy, We wish to appoint someone whom We consider to be useful and suitable, who may govern it with circumspection and direct it to good effect; and as much as you claim the perpetual vicariate of Kirkaldy in the diocese of St. Andrews, and since by your resignation or entry into religion or for whtever reason it has been made vacant, its reversal to Our dear son Robert Shanwell, clerk of this same diocese of St. Andrews, has been reserved by Apostolic authority among the other posts you occupy;

and since We have received trustworthy testimonies about you, concerning your zeal for religion, shamefastness of life, honesty of morals, provision of spiritual things, careful consideration of temporal things, and other benefits of many virtues, We hope you wil be able to be particularly useful and advantageous to the same monastery; and We absolve you now and for the future from whatever sentences of excommunication, suspension, interdict, and any other ecclesiastical sentence, censures snd penalties imposed on you by right or man on whatever occasion and for whatever reason, if any have imposed on you in any way, in as far as this agrees with the effect of the present letters;

and by Apostolic authority We appoint you to the aforesaid monastery, (whose fruits, revenues, and incomes are assessed in the books of the Apostolic Camera at 300 gold florins,) whether it has freely been made vacant by decree or in some other way or by some other person, or by the similar resignation of the said Thomas, or of anyone else from the aforesaid rule and administration, in the Roman Curia, or outwith the Curia, in the presence of a notary and witnesses; because its provision, according to the statutes of the Lateran Council or other canonical sanctions, has been legally evolved upon the Apostolic See and, for whatever reason, pertains particularly and generally to that See, and has usually been disposed, or should be disposed, by that See in consistory;

and respecting its rule and administration, some people have brought a lawsuit whose status by these presents We expressly wish to be considered undecided, as long as provision has not been made canonically in the mean time for you to become abbot of the same monastery without having expressly professed yourself a member of the aforesaid Order.

We appoint you abbot, and commit you to the cure, rule, and administration of that same monastery, with full powers over its spiritual and temporal affairs. We are sending Apostolic documents concerning this to Our venerable brothers, the bishops of Castellimaris and Aberdeen, and to Our dear son the Abbot of Newbattle Monastery in the diocese of St. Andrews, so that one or both of them, assisting you by Our authority to obtain possession in the case of the aforesaid rule and administration and of the property of the said Monastery of Kinloss, by themselves, or by someone else, or by some other people, may ensure the obedience and reverence which are owed and due to you by the aforesaid [monastery], and that Our dear sons, vassals, and other inferiors of the same Monastery of Kinloss render you without reserve the acustomed services and rights which they owe you;

and furthermore that if you be suitable and there is no obstacle from another canon rule, they may receive you, by Our authority, as a monk and a brother in the said Monastery of Kinloss, and clothe you in the monastic habit according to the custom of the monastery; and furthermore that you may make the usual monastic profession by means of those same monks, if you freely wish to do so at their hands, or by the hands of someone else; and by Our said authority they may receive you and admit you, making you to be treated in that place in sincere charity of the Lord.

Those who oppose this will be subject to ecclesiastical censure, their appeal set aside, and silence imposed on them, notithstandng the Apostolic constitution of Pope Boniface VIII, Our predecessor of pious memory, and other Apostolic constitutions of the aforesaid monastery and Order, statutes and customs confirned by oath, Apostolic confirmation, or any other surety; and other privileges and Apostolic indults granted by the aforesaid Cistercian Order abd monastery of Kinloss, and to any other monasteries of the same Cistercian Order and persons belonging to them by Eugene IV of pious memory, Martin V, Nicholas V, Calictus III, Pius II, Sixtus IV and Innocent VIII, and any other Roman Pontiffs, Our predecessors, and the said See, by way of perpetual statute or agreement; or from any other causes, under whatever conditions and forms, and with whatever modifications and other more effective and clauses contrary to custom and other invalidating decrees; and of their own volition, from certain knowledge, and from the plentitude of Apostolic power, in consistory and however else, granted, approved, and renewed on repeated occasions, and observed at anytime, long ago or immemorial;

even if in the aforesaid statutes it be expressly warned that no one can be advanced and appointed to the abbacy of a monastery of the said Cistercian Order unless he shall have been qualified by at least one whole years's probation in the said Order, and according to the monastic regulations of the said Cistercian Order, confirmed by the said authority; and has made his monastic profession in it and worn the habit of a monk.

Apart from this, the appointments connected with the post and any other regulations concerning them have been made by the present See, unless express limits in mode and form have rendered them of no force or effect, and unless it has been provided by the same See that the congregations and persons of those same monasteries - otherwise than is mentioned earlier - of whatever dignity, status, grade, rank, or condition they may be, are not at all obliged to give their obedience, or are unwillingly compelled thereto; they cannot be subject to interdict, suspension, or excommunication, and sentences which run contrary to the force of provisions of this kind are held to be of no force or effect;

and the superiors of the aforesaid congregation of the said Cistercian Order, or their commissioner for the time being, provisions and appointments of this kind notwithstanding, can proceed to elections and confirmation of elections held for the time being according to the monastic ordinances and laudable customs, and the privileges and aforesaid indults of the said Cistercian Order; and, however a vacancy has occurred in these monasteries, once the Father Abbots of this Cistercian Order have been summoned they should proceed to election without impediment, the electors beng persons of these same monasteries expressly professed according to the Cistercian Order.

If these same congregations make no effort to elect, the right of appointment to the said monasteries according to those rights shall devolve upon the Father Abbots present at the time; and those statutes, privileges, and indults cannot be modified by any Apostolic letters containing modifying clauses contrary to custom, nor can their effect be hindered thereby; nor are they esteemed a modification unless a modification of this kind be made in consistory and communicated after a certain time by various letters to the Father Abbot for the time being of the Cistercian Monastery in the diocese of Cabilonensis, and to the Gereral Chapter of the said Cistercian Order, and to the definitors of the same Chapter; and if modification is necessary, even with notice of the fact given, a modification of this kind cannot be granted at all unless it has been made with the agreement of the abbot and congregation of the Cistercian monastery in question; but with regard to all these conditions of theirs, specific, express or some other individual mention must be made of them, not general clauses conveying the same thing; or some other detailed form must be employed for this; and if nothing, word for word, has been omitted in the body of the text and the traditional form has been observed in them; and if the conditions of this kind have been expressed reliably and have been included in full, and will be valid on this occasion as far as they have been given particular and express wording, We permit the changes to be made, whether Apostolic documents have perhaps been sent concerning something else or other things in the said Monastery of Kinloss, or the said See has directed to the congregation of the said Monastery of Kinloss and its vassals and inferiors aforesaid, or to any others, communally or individually, an indult that says that they cannot be subject to interdict, suspension, or excommunication by Apostolic letters which do not make full and express mention, word for word, of an indult of this kind.

We decree that although you have not taken the habit which the monks of Kinloss are accustomed to wear, nor made your monastic profession, you may assume charge, while still a secular clerk, of the rule, administration, and peaceful possession of the aforesaid property for six months, counted from the day of your assuming control, and rule and govern it in spiritual and temporal matters; furthermore, after you have attained peaceful possession of the aforesaid appointment and charge, in spite of being a secular, and the rule and administration of that same property, and have taken the habit and made your profession in the presence of the aforesaid people, you may retain the aforesaid vicarage whos fruits, revenues, and incomes together and individually - except for 4 pounds sterling, which are reserved for you for the maintenance of the burdens of the same vicarage because of the exercise of the cure of incumbent souls - have been reserved by the aforesaid authority for the aforesaid Robert who is to receive annually, their annual value being worth not more, as you assert, than 20 pounds sterling according to the common estimate; this you may have for as long as you live, together with the said Monastery of Kinloss, with the said compensation, for as long as you are in charge of it, with the express agreement of Robert Shanwell, made by the same John, the proctor especially apointed by him for this purpose;

and We grant, as a special favour, by the aforesaid Apostolic authority of these presents, that you may licitly receive, from whichever catholic bishop you prefer, he being in the grace of and communion with the same See, the gift of the benediction of the Gereral Council, by whatever other constitutions, Apostolic ordinances, and statutes and customs (as mentioned previously), together with privileges and indults confirmed by the aforesaid letters, other things to the contrary notwithstanding; and We grant to the same bishop that he may licitly bestow on you the aforesaid gift, and We decree that meanwhile the aforesaid vicarage shall not be vacant, and that it is invalid and idle for anyone, relying upon whatever authority, knowingly or ingnorantly, to call this in question; and we wish that the said vicarage be not deprived of the offices due to it and that its cure of souls be not neglected in any way, but that its accustomed burdens be supported;

and that within the aforesaid six months you will have taken the habit and made your profession in the presence of the aforesaid men. Otherwise, after the elapse of the said six monts, the Monastery of Kinloss will thereby be considered vacant.

Given at Viterbo, 4th July 1528, in the fifth year of Our pontificate.

4. Pope Clement VII to Robert Reid, 16th October 1531

Clement etc. to his dear son Robert Reid, Abbot of the Monastery of Kinloss of the Cistercian Order in the diocese of Moray, greeting etc.

We are persuaded by the clamorous merits of your devotion to Us and to the Apostolic See to look with favour on and grant to you those things which We see will be apt to your benefit. Since, therefore, the office of Prior of Beauly (which means 'Beautiful place') of the Order of Val de Choux in the diocese of Ross was assuredly left vacant and, (its tenure, rule, and governance being in the of Apostolic authority, and transferred from the Order of St. Augustine to the Order of Val de Choux), it was conferred on Our dear son Baledoun, canon of the Order of St. Augustine; and he then or subsequently may have extended the period of vacancy beyond more than one deadline, a postponement which may not yet be finished;

the said James has surrendered into Our hands through Our dear son John Thornton, canon of Moray, the proctor especially appointed by him for this purpose, the gift of the perpetual vicariate of the parish churches of Grantily and Dungeldy of the same diocese, (always taken as one unit), which was being held by Our dear son Adam Muir. The underwritten reversion of this made by you to the said authority had been granted to him by way of exchange for the said office of prior, otherwise it would not be bestowed on him by Us. But he has wilingly surrendered it and We have permitted this surrender; and by this surrender of the vicarages which had been bestowed on him earlier, he left them vacant; and be it known that they are vacant at present. We accept this resignation and surrender and, by other Our letters, We bestow the aforesaid vicarages, made vacant by this same resignation and reserved to Apostolic disposition, upon the aforesaid James for as long as he lives, to raise due, rule, and govern, in as far as is contained in greater detail in those same letters addressed to him.

Since We, by the said authority, had appointed you, now canon of Moray, to the vacant post of abbot of the Monastery of Kinloss of the Cistercian Order in the diocese of Moray, when you had not taken the habit customarily worn by the monks of that same monastery, and had not yet made the monastic profession usually made by those same monks, but were secular clerk; and We decreed that you might hold the post of abbot for a fixed and specified time, and that after you had taken peaceful possession of the charge and the appointment, in spite of being a secular, and assumed charge of the rule and administration and property of the said monastery; and had taken the habit and made your profession in the presence of the aforesaid men; you were to have the power, by dispensation, to retain the perpetual vicariate of the parish church of Kirkcaldy in the diocese of St. Andrews, which formerly you held for life, together with the said monastery for as long as you were in charge of it; and you had resigned freely and willingly into Our hands the canonry and subdeanery, the nominal prebend of the Moray church, and the aforesaid vicarage, and the vicariate severally and combined of the churches you were holding by Apostolic dispensation; and We, accepting this resignation of the canonry and prebend, had bestowed on Our dear son William Paterson, canon of this Moray church, by reason of the resignation of the vicariate of the united churches then made vacant by the aforesaid oath, all and each of the fruits, revenues, and incomes of the canonry, prebend, and vicariate of the aforesaid churches held by you for as long as you lived, in your name and authority;

and after you had taken the aforesaid peaceful possession, together with the monastery for as long as you remained in charge of it, We reserved by Our letters the levying and raising [of the fruits, revenues, and incomes] of the vicariate of the church of Kirkcaldy; We have granted and do assign to you the canonry, prebend, and vicariate of the united churches, these aforesaid being vacant by William on oath;

and because these yield, surrender, and give themselves up to the aforesaid See, you may have free reversal to the same canonry, prebend, and aforesaid vicariate of the united churches, and hold them in commendam for as long as you live, togther with the monastery; and We have granted you the indulgence of also retaining the vicarage of Kirkcaldy in commendam at present; and in recognition of your particular merits, We wish to grant you the special favour of possessing the fruits of the canonry and prebend, so that you will be able to maintain your estate and dignity as Abbot without the need to have recourse to any other financial assistance; and We absolve you now and for the future from whatever sentences of excommunication, suspension, interdict, and any other ecclesiastical sentences, censures, and penalties imposed on you by right or man on whatever occasion and for whatever reason, if any have been imposed on you in any way, in as far as this agrees with the effect of the present letters;

furthermore We grant expressly by these presents the true annual values of the aforesaid fruits, revenues, and incomes of the aforesaid monastery, vicarage of Kirkcaldy, canonry, and prebend, and We have the true final mode of appointment to the office of prior, (even if some general reservation of it in clause [10] in the body of the law is in disagreement); and the attached fruits, revenues, and incomes of the aforesaid office of prior (which is conventual), even if there is some general reservation of appointment to it in clause 10 of the body of the law, their annual worth, according to common assessment, being a sum not exceeding 40 pounds sterling, as you claim; in whatever way [it has been vacated], or from whomsoever, or by the free resignation, freely made of someone from it, in the Roman Curia, or outwith the Curia in the presence of a public notary and witnesses, or according to the constitution of Pope John XXII, Our predecessor of happy memory, which begins Execrabilis, or because of the pursuit of another ecclesiastical benefice associated with it by whatever authority, or because the said James has not been transferred from the Order of St. Augustine to the Order of Val de Choux within the last time specified for his being able to hold the office; and if it has been vacant for such a long time that its bestowal has legally been devolved upon the Holy See according to the statutes of the Lateran Council.

This office of prior is specifically reserved to Apostolic disposition, or generally reserved, because (as was said above) it is conventual, and those who take office have usually been elected thereto, and the office has a jurisdictional cure of souls attached to it. The lawsuit between the said James and another or others in the said Curia, or outwith the Curia in the presence of a judge or judges who are the regular or designated hearer of causes in the Palace, and whose status (along with the names and surnames of both judges and litigants We wish, by these presents, to be placed at Our disposal) is expressly to remain undecided as long as the right which is being sought has not be awarded specifically to anyone.

We grant this office to you, with all its attached rights and appurtenances, for as long as you live, together with the monastery, the vicarage of Kirkcaldy, and the fruits of the canonry and prebend reserved for you; or in the event of a reversal to those men, the holding, rule, and governance of them since the aforesid canonry and prebend have been granted to you; and We permit you, regarding the residual fruits, revenues, and incomes usually needed to support the burdens of the office of prior, to dispose and regulate them, just as those who have the title to them for the time being have been able to dispose and regulate them, or should have done so; but We entrust this to you unreservedly by aliention of whatever removable property and movable valuables belong to this same office of prior, under threat of ecclesiiastical sanction;

and the said office of prior being the subject of litigation, as long as you have not trespassed in and upon every right to which this James was seeking claim or might meek claim in the same office of prior, We, by the aforesaid Apostolic power, remove the said right and grant it to you; and We induct you, by the same authority, to this right and to the prosecution and defence of the aforesaid lawsuit and cause, at the same point at which James was at the time of his resignation and, had he not resigned, at which he could and should have been admitted to the office of prior; and We decree that if the judge or judges in whose presence this lawsuit is being heard do not make a decision for one or for any of the co-litigants, then it will be adjudged and should be adjudged in your favour by these same judges as far as it will have been legally decided to permit you to persue this right in their presence.

We have instructed Our venerable brothers, the Bishops of Casertana and Aberdeen, by Apostolic document, to receive you either together or one by himself or using a deputy or deputies, and when an oath of due obedience has been taken in Our name and that of the Roman Church, according to the term we send in Our bull Introclusam , by you or your proctor in your name, to induct you by Our authority into pssession of the office of prior and of the attached rights and aforesaid appurtenances, and defend you once you have been inducted, any illicit obstacles thereto have been removed; and causing you, or the aforesaid proctor on your behalf, to be admitted to the office of prior according to custom, and to be entirely answerable for you and the fruits, revenues, and incomes, rights and obventions of the office and such things as are attached to it, by restraining objectors thereto by means of ecclesiastical censure with a summons added, notwithstanding the constitution of Pope Boniface VIII, Our predecessor of pious memory, and other Apostolic constitutions; and notwithstanding statutes confirmed by oath, Apostolic confirmation, or any other surety, or whatever the contrary customs of the monastery or other religious house from which the said office of prior may be dependent, and of their office of prior and of the Order of Val de Choux;

or if they have obtained general letters concerning the provisions or appointments to be made by him to the offices of prior, or special letters from the said See or its legates concerning other ecclesiastical benefices in these parts; and even if, by the authority of these, the matter has proceeded to inhibition, reservation, decree, or has proceeded in any other fashion; in all such cases We wish that you be granted precedence in pursuit of the said office of prior or other benefices; or to Our venerable brother, the Bishop of Ross, or Our dear sons; the congregation of the priory, or to anyone else generally or individually;

therefore the same See grants as an indulgence that they may not be bound at all to the reception of provision of anyone else, nor can they be compelled or subject to interdict, suspension or excommunication to do so; and with respect to the appointment, provision, presentation, election, or whatever other disposition, conjointly or separately, of the offices of prior and any other ecclesiastical benefices, there can be no provision, nor can there be any such granted, by Apostolic letters which do not make full, express, word for word mention of this indult; nor by any other indulgences of the said See, general or particular, however worded, which do not express or include it in full as in these presents, may the effect of this favour be impeded or deferred; and there must be particular mention of each, fully expressed, in Our letters, with the proviso that the said office of prior be not deprived of the offices which are du to it, and the cure of souls attached to it be in no way neglected, but its aforesaid burdens be supported accordingly.

We declare it henceforth invalid and idle for anyone, relying upon whatever authority, knowingly or ignorantly, to call this in question; and let no one be permitted to oppose his document of Our absoution, appointment, substitution, retirement, departure, decree, command, and will; but if anyone presumes to make such an attempt, let him know he will have incurrred the anger of Almighty God and of the blessed Apostles, Peter and Paul.

Given at Rome, at St. Peter's, 16th October 1531, in the eighth year of Our pontifiate.

5. Pope Paul III to Robert Reid, 20th July 1541

Paul etc. to his dear son Robert, [Bishop] Elect of Orkney, greeting.

The office of the Papacy having been committed to Us from on high, even though Our merits are not equal to it, We preside over the government of all churches and, with the Lord's help, We are anxious to perform that office usefully. We are moved that when it comes to the government of these churches, We take care to appoint to them such shepherds as know how to instruct the people of their cure, who have been entrusted to them, not only by means of teaching them the Word, but by example of good work; and who wish and are able to rule and govern the churches committed to them profitably and happily in a state of peace and tranquillity;

for some time We have reserved to Our ordination and disposition the appointments of all churches vacant, declaring that henceforth it is invalid and idle for anyone, relying upon any authority, knowingly or ignorantly, to call this in question. By the death of Robert, Bishop of Orkney, of good memory, who presided over the church of Orkney while he lived and died away from the Roman Curia, the consolation of a shepherd is now missing, as we understand from trustworthy informants; with respect for a swift and happy provision for this church, (which no one save Ourself coud or can dispose on this occasion, the abovesaid reservation and decree not withstanding), lest the church be subject to the inconvenieces of a long vacancy, We have given the matter paternal and careful study, and after careful consideration with Our brethren about the appointment of a useful and fruitful person to this church, We have at last directed Our attention to you, the appointed Abbot of the Monastery of the Blessed Virgin Mary of Kinloss, of the Cistercian Order, in the diocese of Moray, and a member of the priesthood; and Our most dear son in Christ, James, illustrious King of Scots, has given Us counsel, and has by letters addressed humble supplication to Us on this same matter.

Learning, purity of life, honesty of morals, foresight in spiritual matters and circumspection in temporal, and other gifts of many virtue have been ascribed to you by trustworthy testimonies; all of which, because of th claim of your virtues, both We and Our brethren have weighed in due thought, along with the advice of the brethren of the aforesaid church; and by Apostolic authoity We appoint and prefer you to the office of bishop, to the pastorate, cure, and administration of that church, and commit to you full powers in both spiritual and temporal matters; in such manner that you realise that you are not, in consequence, to cease being in charge of the said monastery whose charge you have, but as you presided over the said monastery as abbot for as long as you lived, so you preside over your church as bishop; and you are head and pastor of your church and also true abbot of the aforesaid monastery.

We trust in him who gives thanks and dispenses rewards that, with the Lord's directing your acts, he aforesaid church will be ruled usefully by your happy governance, and will be directed prosperously, and will receive happy increase in those same spiritual and temporal things. Therefore, taking with prompt devotion the yoke of the Lord imposed on your shoulder, study so to excercise the aforesaid cure and administration carefully, faithfully, and prudently, that it may be a source of joy that this church has been committed to a provident governor and a faithful administrator, and you may thence merit Our benediction and the benediction of the Holy See as a reward of eternal thanks and grace to follow more abundantly.

Given at Rome, at Santa maria [Maggiore], 16th October, 1541, in the seventh year [of Our pontificate.]

6. Pope Paul III to Robert Reid, 16th October, 1541

Paul etc. to his dear son Robert, [Bishop] Elect of Orkney, greetings etc.

Acknowledging your personal devotion to Us and to the Holy See, and recognising the claims of your merits, We concede to you by Our favour those things which We see will be conducive to your benefit. Therefore today We have heeded the claims of your virtues and the advice of Our brethren, and by Apostolic authority have appointed you, formerly Abbot of the Monastery of the Blessed Virgin Mary of Kinloss, of the Cistercian Order, in the diocese of Moray, to be bishop and shepherd of the church in Orkney which was in need of the consolation of a shepherd, in such manner that you did not cease to be in charge of the said monastery whose charge you had, but as you have presided over the said monastery as abbot for as long as you lived, so you were to preside over your church as bishop, and were head of your church and the true abbot of this monastery, as is contained in further detail in the letters We have written;

and just as We have allowed by Apostolic dispensation that you held the office of prior of the aforesaid charge and appointment of Beauly of the Order of Val de Choux, and the perpetual vicariate of the parish church of Kirkcaldy in the diocese of Ross and St. Andrews, in as much as you have all and each of the fruits, revenues, and incomes of the canonry and sub-deanery of the declared prebend of the church of Moray for as long as you live, together withthe aforesaid monastery, office of prior, and vicariates, in as far as your powers of levying, exacting, and raising have been reserved by the said authority; and by the same authority you have been granted the reversals to them with respect of the canonry and prebend under certain express circumstances; so that you may hold the estate of bishop with the more becoming dignity that the office demands, We grant that you may seek the assistance of extra revenue, and in recognition of your aforementioned merits, We wish to grant you special favour;

and We absolve you now and for the future from whatever sentences of excommuniction, suspension, interdict, and any other ecclesistical sentence, censure, and penalties imposed on you by right or man on whatever occasion and for whatever reason, if any have been imposed on you in any way, in as far as this agrees with the effect of the present letters; and We decree of Our own will, (not because of your entreaty or that of anyone else, in offering a petition to Us about this matter), and of Our undiluted liberality We grant that after you have taken peaceful possession of the aforesaid charge and appointment of the rule and administration of the church in Orkney and of its property, or the greater part thereof, and have received the gift of consecration; you may freely and licitly retain the office of prior (which is recognised as conventual), and its fruits, revenues, and incomes minus and annual pension of 120 merks Scots coin and 8 pounds sterling paid annually by the said authority to Our dear son James Baldwyn, canon of the Order of St. Augustine;

as We have allowed reservations and this vicarage in connection with which, in certain circumstances, express compensation has been similarly granted by the aforesaid authority to Our dear son, Robert Shanwell, priest of the aforesaid diocese of St. Andrews; as similarly also We have allowed its fruits, revenues, and incomes, all and severally, by the same authority, to be paid to the same Robert Shanwell for as long as he lives; as also We have allowed that 18 [pounds] have been reserved for the office of prior, which has usually been assumed by election, and its cure of souls, for as long as you live;

these you may retain, together with the church of Orkney and the aforesaid monastery as long as you are in charge of it, together with the fruits, revenues, and incomes of the canonry and prebend, which, according to common assessment, have an annual value not exceeding 14 pounds sterling; these you may receive and levy for as long as you live, as is said above, and may use the aforesaid reversals granted to you and, in that event, acquire the aforesaid canonry and prebend or, as is said above, freely and licitly retain them, the constitutions of the General Council and any other constitutions and Apostolic ordinances, and the statutes of the monastery or other monastic house to which the aforesaid office of prior may be attached, and of the aforesaid office of prior and of the church of Moray and of the [Cistercian] Order, reinforced by oath, Apostolic confirmation or any other surety, and all contrary customs notwithstanding.

By the wording of the presents We grant you our special favour, declaring that the office of prior and the vicarage are not vacant, that the reversal conceded to you is not extinguished, the reservation of their fruits at an end, but not at the expense of the compensation granted to the said Robert Shanwell; and that it is invalid and idle for anyone, relying upon whatever authority, knowingly or ignorantly, to call this in question; and We wish that, in the event of this compensation, the office of prior and vicarage be not deprived of the offices due to them, and that the cure of soul in the vicarage and of the office of prior, should any be attached to it, be not neglected; but that their usual burdens and those of the aforesaid canonry and prebend be properly supported.

Let no one be permitted to infringe or rashly dare to oppose this decree of Our absolution, dispensation, decree, and will. If anyone, however, presumes to make such an attempt, let him know he will have incurred the anger of Almighty God and the Blessed Apostles, Peter and Paul.

Given at Rome, at Santa Maria [Maggiore], 16th, October 1541 in the seventh year [of Our pontificate.]

Appendix 2

Books in the library of Robert Reid

Academia Lovaniensis: Comentarii in Isagogen Porphyrii et omnes libros Aristotelis de Dialectica. Louvain 1553

Alciata, A>Opera. Basle 1557-58

Amalarius: Speculum Antiquae Devotionis, ed.Cochlaeus. Mainz 1549

Ambrosius S>Opera

Antoninus S. (Forciglioni) Chronica, Historiarum Domini Antinii Archipraesulis Florentini Nuper uno nunc quoque et gemino Indice aucta. Lugundi 1543 (or 27 or 12)

Arboreus, Joannes: Commentarii in epistolas. Paris 1553
    Commentarii in Evangelista. Paris 1551

Augustinus SA> de Civitate Dei, de Trinitate

Bartolus: Volumen cum casibus. Lyon 1500

Bembo, Pietro cardinal: Opera. Basle 1556

Bernadus S. Melliflui devotique doctoris sancti Bernadi abbatis clareuallensis Cisterciensis ordinis Opus preclarum suos Complectens sermones de tempore, de sanctis: et super Cantica canticorum. Aliosque complures eius sermones et sententias. Eiusdem in super epistolas: ceteraque universa eius op uscula. Lugundi 1515

Bolzani, Valeriano, Giovanni Piero: Hieroglyphica. Basle 1556

Bonaventua S.D. Eustachii Findensae ep. Albaniensis Autoritatum Sanctarum libri quatuar. Cologne 1542

Broekweg, Antonius, O.F.M. a Konigstein. Evangeliorum Montesaron. Cologne 1542
    In IV Evangelia Enarrationum. Pars proma. Paris 1534

Brunus, Conrad: De Hiereticis. Mainz 1549

Calcagnini, Celio. Opera aliqupt. Basle 1544

Castro, Alfonso de. O.F.M. De Justa Haereticorum Punitione. Lyon 1556

Chrysostomus, Joannes. Opera

Coccio, M.A. Sabellicus: Historiae Rerum Venetarum. Basle 1556

Damascenus, S. Joannes. Opera. Basle 1535

Duns Scotus, Joannes O.F.M. Primus, secundus, sententiarum doctoris subtilis Scoti. Venetiis 1490 (?)

Super Quartum Librum Sententiarum. Paris 1520

Foirciglioi, Antoninus - see Antoninus S.

Genealogia comitum Orcadensis ca. 1433 ms (text is printed P.A.Munch)

George, bisop of Alexandria. J. Chrystostomus Vita. Paris 1552

Graduale (Apud Culross exscriptum) ms

Gratian: Decretum Rhapsodiae. Lyon no date

Gregorius (I?). Sanctu Gregorii Magni Opera. Paris 1518 (or 33 or 42)

Gregorius IX. Decretales Epistole Gregorii Noni Pontificis Maximi, iam recens plus sexcentis mendis cum in textu tum in glossis repurgate. Paris 1527

Herold, Joannes. Orthodoxographid. Basle 1555

Hieronymus S. Liber Epistolarum Sancti Hieronymi. Lyon 1525
    (or 08 or 13) Opera

Isocrates: Orationes omnes. Basle 1548

Leo Magnus pp. Opera. Cologne 1546

Letman, Herman.De instauranda religione. Basle 1544(?)

Lippomano, Luigi. Catena in Exodum. Paris 1550

Maior, Joannes. Sententiae

Milleloquium Augustini. Lyon 1555

Missale (apud Culross exscriptum) ms

Molinaeus, Carolus. Tractatus Commerciorum et Usurarum, Redituumque Pecunia Constitutorum, et Monetarum, cum Nova et Analytica Explicatione. Paris 1555

Munster, Sebastian, Compositii horologiorum. Basle 1531
Optatus: De Donatistiis. Mainz 1549
Panvinio, Onofrio, Veroniensis, F. August. Fasti et Triumphi Romae a Romulo rege usque ad Caolum
    V. Caes. Aug. sive Epitome Regum, Consulum etc. Venetiis 1551
Epitome pontificu Romanerum. Venice 1557
Piero, Giovanni - see Bolzani
Ponisson, Francois: De officiis pastorum. Toulouse 1550
Rituum Ecclesiasticorum Liber. Cologne 1557
Regiam Maieastatum: ms
Rolewinck, Werner: Fasciculus Temporum, omnes antiquorum cronicas complectens. No place of
    printing, no date.
Tapper, Ruard: Declaratio theologorum Loveniensium. Lyon 1554
Theodoretus: In epistolas S. Pauli commentarius nunc primum Latine versus, ed. Gentian Hervet.
    Florence 1557
Thomas Aquinas S> Commentarii in epistolas D. Pauli Summa theologica (Basilon 1485 or Venetiis
    1495 or Nurnburg 1496)
Tiraqueau, Andre: Tractus, Le Mort saisit le Vif. Paris 1554
Ane Tractat of a part of Ynglis Cronikle shawand of ther kings part of thar ewill and cursit governace
    and thar unhappide lynmage, als weil fra autentik writ als fra thar awne fenzeit Policronicon.
    ca 1460 ms (the text is printed: H.M.General Rgister House. Chronicles of the Scots and other
    early memorials of Scottish Histroy. Ed. W.F.Skene LlD. Edinburgh 1867)
Van Zon, Frans: Demonstrationum Religionis Christianae Liber Primus. Antwerp 1556
Vtus ac novum testamentum cum glossis
Viguerius, Joannes, O.P.Institutiones (Theologica)) ad naturalem philosophiam. Paris 1558
Vincenius (Bellovacensis O.P.?) Speculum morale. Venetiis 1493: Speculum naturale, Speculum
    doctrinale, Speculum historiale - all Venetiis 1494 (identification uncertain, all known
    particulars are "4 Vincentii de volumina"; Speculum morale possibly a spurious work by
    Vincent de Beauvais)
Witzel, Georg (Wicelius). Postilla, hoc est, Enarratio Epistolarum et Evangelorum de Tempore et de
    Sanctis. Cologne 1553
Quadragesimales Conciones. Cologne 1555

Attributed to Reid but doubtful

(Qignonez Franc.) Bevarium Romanum. Lyon 1555
("Orchaden" on binding and date the only proof of Reid, binding unlike other books)
Totum Ius pontificium
(no particulars given)

Books owned by Ferrerio, Giovanni "of Piedmont"

Filelfo, Francesco: Elegantes et familiares epistolae. Louvain 1515
Champier, Symphorien: Mirabilium diuinorum volumina quattuor. Lyon 1517
Quintilian: Oratorarium Institutionum libri xii. Paris 1519
Douglas, David: De Naturae Mirabilibus Opusculum. Paris 1524
Poliziano, Angelo: Omnium operum tomus prior. Paris 1526
(a) Probus: De scripturis antiquis. Paris 1531
Valerius Maximus: Opera. Ibid.
Liber Usuum Cisterciensis Ordinis. Paris 1531
Bude, John: Hystory and Cronikilis of Scotland. Edinburgh c.1540
Mirandola, Pico della: De animae immortalitate. Paris 1541
    (Last two given to Henry Sinclair, Bishop of Ross)

Bibliography

S Anderson. "Cardinal of Scotland" (John Donald)
Batten. "Priory of Beauly"
Brunton and Haig. "Senators of the College of Justice"
Calderwood. "History of the Scottish Kirk"
Cant & Firth. "The Light in the North" (Orkney Press)
Cant. "The Constitution of St. Magnus Cathedral" in "Northern Isles Connections" ed. Barbara
    Crawford (BBC)
Craven. "History of the Church in Orkney - prior to 1558 (Wm.Peace & son)
Crawford. "An Unrecogniable Statue" in "Northern Isles Connections" ed. Crawford (Orkney
    Press)
Dickens. "The Age of Hunamism and Reformation" (Prentice-Hall)
Dilworth. "Scottish Monasteries inthe Late Middle Ages" (Edin.Univ.Press)
Donaldson. "Reformed by Bishops" (The Edina Press)
Donaldson. "The Edinburgh History of Scotland" vol.3 (Mercat Press)
Fawcett. "Kirkwall Cathedral: an Architectural Analysis" in "St. Magnus Cathedral and Orkney's
    Twelfth Century Renaissance" ed. Crawford
Ferrerius Pedemontanus. "R. in Christo patri etc." Introduction to Essay on Immortality by Pico
    della Mirandola
Ferrerius. "Historia abbatum - Monasterii A Kinlos"
Grant. "History of the University of Edinburgh" in Cassel's "Old and New Edinburgh"
Hamilton State Papers
Hannay. "The College of Justice: Essays: (stair Soc. 1990)
Hibbert. "Rome: the Biography of a City"
Hossack. "Kirkwall in the Orknies"
Innes Review "Humanism in Scotland"
Jean Seznec. "The Survival of The Pagan Gods" Princeton University Press.
Keith. "Scottish Bishops"
Knox. "History of the Reformation in Scotland"
Letters and Papers of Henry VIII (ed. Gairdner)
Sir David Lindsay. "Ane Pleasant Satyre of the Thrie Estaitis"
Lyndsay of Pitscottie. "Chronicles of Scotland"
Mackenzie. "Lives of Scottish Writers"
Mooney. "The Cathedral and Royal Burgh of Kirkwall" (Mackintosh)
Nowosilski, Leon. "The Life and Times of Robert Reid" MS
Peterkin. "Rentals of Orkney"
Privy Council Minutes 1553
Sadler State Papers
Shaw. "History of Moray"
Smyth. "Chronicles, Book of Kinloss"
Storer Clouston. "History of Orkney" (Mackintosh)
Stuart. "Records of the Monastery of Kinloss"
Tudor. "History of Orkney" (Stanford)
Wallace. "Islands of Orkney"
Wormald. "Court, Kirk and Community" (Edin. Univ. Press)

Index